Just a Couple of Women Talkin’

Dear Jim,

To a dear, dear friend. Thank you for all you taught me.

Terri

Just A Couple of Women Talkin' . . .

The *Real* Story of Being a Woman Entrepreneur

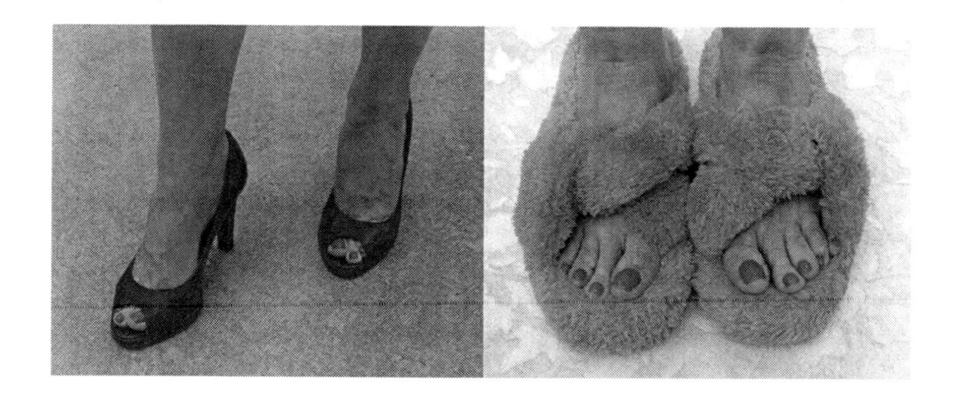

The Journey. The Business. The Shoes.

Terri Bonar-Stewart *and* Linda S. Gravett, Ph.D.

Business Innovation Press
An imprint of Integrated Media Corporation
Louisville, Kentucky

For general information on our other products and services please contact Linda S. Gravett, Ph.D. at P.O. Box 45429, Cincinnati, OH 45254 or online at www.gravett.com.

Printed in the United States of America.
ISBN: 978-0-9832639-7-5
For information, contact: **Integrated Media Corporation 12305 Westport Road, Louisville, KY 40245, 800-944-3995.**

Other books by Dr. Linda Gravett:
HRM Ethics: Perspectives for a New Millennium, 2002, Atomic Dog Publishing, Cincinnati, OH
Bridging the Generation Gap, 2007, Gravett and Throckmorton, Career Press, NY, NY
Using Your Emotional Intelligence to Develop Others, 2009, Caldwell and Gravett, Palgrave-MacMillan, NY, NY

Author photos by Paula Norton, Norton Photography
Hair and make-up for photos by Ken Miskell
Cover photos by E-S Bonita Bonar
Designed by Kelly Elliott
Edited by Florence Huffman

A portion of the profits from this book will be donated to support the YWCA of Cincinnati and to Bad Girl Ventures, a micro-financing and education organization targeting women entrepreneurs.

Extraordinary Acclaim for
Just a Couple of Women Talkin'

I am so excited to become a consultant, but this . . . made me realize that I cannot walk off the stage of graduation and enter the world as a consultant. Who would hire a recent graduate with zero consulting experience? Now I am looking for an avenue by which to gain experience.

—Graduate student

The instrument indicates to me that I may be better suited in continuing internal consulting roles rather than the role of solo practitioner.

—Practicing internal consultant

I have occasionally considered consulting; but I recognize that while I like mentoring and being an "expert," I don't ask people enough questions. I'll leave consulting to those of you who really like to probe.

—Professional HR manager

Dedication

This book is dedicated to the hundreds of smart, savvy, hard-working women who've been my role models and mentors over the years (you know who you are). Thank you for reaching out to me and helping me keep it real, and for giving me a hug when I needed a hug, and a kick in the pants when that's what was necessary.

Linda

For my late father, Cliff Bonar Jr., for teaching me about entrepreneurship and what life is really all about, and my late mother, Delores Lawson Bonar Lenara, for teaching me to trust my intuition and how to manage.

To my sisters Linda, Darla, and Bonny for their continuous random acts of love; my husband, Thomas S. Williams, for his patience, his stories, and mostly, his unconditional love; and my son and future entrepreneur, Ashley Stewart.

To George Manning and Alan Weiss for encouraging me to write this book.

With love and gratitude,
Terri

Acknowledgments

Thanks to Vicki Casto, Debby Combs, Maggie Frye, Nancy Waldeck, Bobby Clark, Ron Jackson, Bonny Bonar, and Linda Wiese, for reading drafts of this manuscript and suggesting changes that made the book better.

Geoffrey M. Bellman
(George) Marty Berry
Albert Bandura
Cliff Bonar, Jr.
Albert Einstein
Angie Taylor
Ashley Bonar Stewart
Becky Timberlake
Tina Sharp
Charles Handy
Darla B. Kettenacker
De Stewart
Delores Lawson Bonar Lenara
Don Harden
E-S Bonita Bonar
Edna Flaugher
Edward A. Harvey
Ella Mae Sorrell Mayes
George Manning
Jack Nimersheim
Jeff Thurman
Jim Moon
Jim Steinke
Judith Clabes
Kenneth Stewart, Sr.
LaVada Stewart
Linda B. Wiese
Linda Gill
Luce Bonar
Mary Parker Follett
Michael J. Posey
Nanci Bonar
Nancy Shellhous Conner
Pam Beigh
Renee Whitehead Springer
Sr. Mary Andrea Simpson
Susan Calloway Nimersheim
Thomas S. Williams
Alan Weiss
Walter Black
Frances Hesselbein
Therese Williams
Jim Collins
Andrea Gabor
Candace Kendle
Mike Green
Clayton M. Christensen
Joy Galbraith
Guy Kawasaki
Mary Cay Ostendorf
Vicky Rainey

And, the inspirational students of the Urban Learning Center.

Table of Contents

PREFACE

BEFORE YOU START READING THE BOOK . . .

If you are ready to start your own consulting business, then what we say in the first three chapters may influence you to move ahead more quickly. If you are not ready to start your own business, these chapters will not convince you to start your business; however, the ensuing chapters may, because starting and building your consulting business is not all about the numbers. For us, consulting has been a calling—a natural evolution—a decision that came from our gut—intuition—whatever you call that feeling that you get when you know you have chosen the right path.

So, if you have that "feeling," then proceed at random through this book. If you just need that little boost to justify that feeling, then start at the beginning. We think you will laugh a bit at where we have been, but hopefully, not where we are going. We think some of you may even cry. Our intention is to give you the real story of two journeys as recollected over kitchen table conversations, with just a bit of Tai Chi and qigong principles thrown in for good measure.

We certainly have enjoyed creating this book; we hope you enjoy reading it.

Linda Gravett
Terri Bonar-Stewart
2011

INTRODUCTION

COFFEE SHOP TALK AND KITCHEN TABLE CONVERSATIONS

We were sitting in our favorite coffee shop, just enjoying the coffee and our rare time together as friends and colleagues. We'd known each other for probably ten years and had some great conversations about consulting, running a business, and balancing full lives. One morning, we both had an epiphany: why not put down all of our great conversations into a book?! We decided to mull it over and discuss the idea more seriously the next time we met for coffee.

A few months later, we took time out from our hectic schedules to catch up with each other again. Linda was wrapping up another book and was definitely intrigued by the idea of writing a book on consulting, and more specifically, a book from a woman's perspective. Terri was completing a long-term client project and had so many ideas in her head, she was "bursting at the seams" to get those ideas on paper to share with other women. We thought, "It's time . . . it's time for an informal, down-to-earth look at the state of women-owned businesses in today's society and a realistic perspective on what it takes to start and build a consulting practice." We wanted this book to have the feel of "just a couple of women talking" over coffee.

As we began to write this book, we found the experience to be an opportunity to be more reflective than we anticipated, sometimes even cathartic. Linda had a difficult time, at first, writing in a personal, conversational style because her previous books were in a more formal, "business-y" style. To be truly helpful for women readers though, Linda knew that she'd have to open up and be very candid about the problems, challenges and issues she had to deal with to take the risk to start, build and sustain a consulting business. For Terri, the challenge was actually writing her first book.

Writing a book is the equivalent of learning a new private language, working in a new industry, and testing new skills all at once. Linda, as a published author, was the bright light on the path to a new adventure for Terri. You'll find both our personal stories interwoven throughout this book, and our hope is that you'll see yourself in those stories.

More than anything, this book is our way of encouraging women who are considering consulting to do their homework and learn what consulting is—and isn't—and go into (or choose not to go into) the venture with their eyes wide open. We both love consulting and have found successful paths – we want to encourage other women to find their own path to success and fulfillment. You'll find information in this book about the mechanics of starting a consulting business, yet the main emphasis is on the personal journeys we both followed, and are still following, to achieve our dreams. We'll share stories about ourselves, our families, and some of our favorite clients. The stories about our clients are shared with their permission, and we appreciate their willingness to be a part of this endeavor.

1

Finding Your Passion and Your Power

Awareness is the first step. Attention second. Action third.
—Terri Bonar-Stewart, 2011

There is power in one. I can be that one and be a force.
I can join others and be awesome.
—Linda S. Gravett, 2011

There are no ordinary women, but some women have yet to find their passion and power. Some will become entrepreneurs; some will become consultants. This book is for the women who are considering consulting as a profession and the option to move to a business of their own.

Most of us have the desire to change the world. Few of us have the desire to endure the risky journey to make that change happen. When the craving to change our world overcomes the anticipated risks, people say that we are passionate about what we do.

Passion can begin anywhere, from . . .

- The pain that results from a calamity: "I don't want that to happen to anyone else."
- The pleasure: "I want everyone to be able to enjoy this."
- An internal sense of right and wrong: "Everyone deserves an education."
- A mindset of scarcity: "I want to make a lot of money because my mother gave up her career for her family."
- An attitude of abundance: "There is so much beauty in creating something new from something old."
- A tradition: "My mother did it; my grandmother did it, now it is my turn to do it."
- A "calling": "Answering and giving voice to the internal search for meaning and purpose in our lives."

An obsessive desire to change the world grows from the roots of passion.

Now, if we have the power to do it . . .

Power comes from confidence, restlessness, and thousands of bits and bytes of experience and information. We all possess the power. Some of us have simply not found it yet within ourselves.

But when we do . . .

Together passion and power form potential—an energy that bounces around in your head like a perpetual rubber ball—until you discover the right sliver of opportunity. When that energy is focused, it becomes a driving force to create. An increasing number of women choose a business of their own as the creative outlet.

Crafters or consultants, plumbers or performers, retail gurus or reclamation specialists, each has her desire, and her dream to fulfill. Many women recognize opportunities not taken by others, ideas that others ignore, and combinations of ideas that others think unlikely candidates for business opportunities.

When we are considering a major change in our lives, we experience internal conflict. Terri refers to this inner conflict as anticipatory dissonance. That dissonance—that discomfort—creates pressure to either maintain the status quo or change it. When we chose change, the pressure can ignite an inner fire from which a business concept can flare.

The desire becomes stronger, forming a powerful thrust to "do something about it." Conception has taken place, then an infant is born. Like a newborn, the force becomes consuming—a dependent idea—leaning on you – depending upon you for food, for comfort, for attention. Soon the new "baby idea" has become a toddler and begins to explore all the avenues of independence. Little Ms. Personality is hiding behind every couch, playing peek-a-boo around every corner, giggling down the hallways of your mind. It is time to share her picture, and expose her to other "Little Miss Personalities."

We found our passion and the power to become human resource consultants in Midwest, USA, over seventeen years ago.

The format we will use for sharing our experiences is based on our own observations of consulting, our stories of pain and pleasure, and actual applications of what we learned, then some final cheerleading comments for those of you who wish to join us.

WHY READ THIS BOOK?

The nature of women is to share and collaborate and to make the path easier for those who follow. We have filled a big bowl of bright stories, reflective memories and lessons learned.

Amid this big bowl of stories and experiences, maybe you will find one or two that speak to you – that cause your own Aha! moment, or even provide a bit of inspiration. Our desire to share this with you is an exercise of our passion about what we chose to do with our lives.

We encourage you to give yourself permission to embark on your own journey. Don't let anyone or anything stop you once you have found your passion and your power.

If you want to stay where you are—then do it.

But, if you want a business that provides simply for your own lifestyle needs, then don't be cowed by those who seek to minimize what you desire to do. Become a "Lifestyle Entrepreneur."

If you want to build a global market in a new enterprising area—then do it. Don't let anyone tell you that you can't do it. Become a "Global Mogul."

If you want to build a totally new business that doesn't even have a market yet—then do it. Become an "Innovation Tycoon."

We don't know you personally, but we know enough women who overcame obstacles bigger than those we faced and they did it. They were, in part, our own inspiration. So, begin to follow your dream, your passion and to do it with aplomb.

"You cannot plough a field by turning it over in your mind."

—Anonymous

2

Our Slips Were Showing

USED TO BE OUR SLIPS WERE SHOWING . . .

Terri

I was "almost fourteen" when I met the first man of my dreams, and much to my mother's chagrin, he was eighteen. Our dates consisted of dreamy-eyed conversations – limited to the schoolyard – and in plain sight of the entire small town. (In the early 1960s, dates did not mean kissing, or touching in any way.) In a rare moment of temporary insanity, my mother did allow me to go to his high school graduation in the school gym across the street from where I lived.

I remember that it was the first time I wore three-inch heels and a hand-me-down suit with a pencil-cut skirt from my Aunt Ella Mae. I must have been some sight—thirteen years old, wobbling across the street in my first spiked heels and tight skirt. I thought I was all grown up.

As I walked out the door, my wary mother only had one thing to say: "Your slip is showing."[i]

≈

i For those young women who might not know, slips are those silk or nylon undergarments, usually with lace trim, that kept you from being able to see through the thick cotton or wool garments that were our primary layer of clothing. The lace was just in case the slip showed, or you were one of "those girls" trying to be seductive. And you wondered why Madonna was scandalous in wearing her underwear as her only clothing. It is all relative.

WOMEN USED TO TALK ABOUT THAT—HAVING OUR SLIPS SHOW. NOW WHAT IS SHOWING IS OUR IMPACT.

Just ten years after Terri's schoolyard romance, the US Census report indicated that "women-owned business accounted for 4.6 percent of all firms in the United States with receipts from women-owned firms making up only.03 percent of all business receipts in the United States."[1]

THE SLIP THAT WAS SHOWING IS GROWING

In Kentucky, where Terri lives and operates her business, the Small Business Administration reports 25.6 percent of businesses were women-owned in 2007—with an increase of 7.5 percent from 2000 to 2008. In Ohio, where Linda lives and operates her business 27.7 percent of businesses were women-owned in 2007 with an increase of 8.3 percent from 2000 to 2008. (Authors' note: We understand that these numbers appear inconsistent and are reported for the years of 2007 and 2008, however, this is how the SBA has reported the data. The national survey was conducted 2007 and reported in 2008.)

Both Kentucky and Ohio are below the national average. California, Texas, New York, Florida and Illinois are the top five states for women-business ownership and help bring the national average to 28.7 percent.

Combined with equally-owned firms (50 percent male ownership; 50 percent female ownership) the numbers are 45.2 percent in Kentucky and 42.7 percent for Ohio, an increase of 68.3 percent from 2000 to-2008, and 66.5 percent from 2000 to 2008, respectively.[2]

The American Express Report on the State of Women-Owned Businesses Report (2011) indicates that women- and equally-owned firms together represent 46 percent of U.S. firms.

THE GLOBAL CONSULTING MARKET—OUR INDUSTRY

The market for global consulting is estimated to be 366 billion U.S. dollars in 2011.[3] The Human Resource consulting market is estimated at 12.2 billion dollars and the strategic management market at 26.5 billion dollars in 2011.[4]

Figure 1.1 depicts the global consulting marketplace. The asterisk represents the home base of our firms, Gravett and Associates and Just The Basics® Inc.

OUR MARKET DOMAIN

Each of us operates a human resource consulting practice based in the Midwest, United States. Additionally, Linda does business outside the United States, often in Japan, a country where she lived for several years (she speaks the language). And, we are committed to spreading the word about the value of women as consultants throughout the known universe. There is plenty of room for good consultants.

THE SMALL BUSINESS MARKETPLACE

Throughout this book, we have chosen to focus on smaller consulting practices. We know about small businesses because we each own and operate one. Additionally, there is a wealth of published information on larger consulting practices. For more information on the largest consulting firms, www.kennedyinfo.com and www.plunkettresearch.com provide significant research data.

Terri

While traveling, I once sat next to a gentleman on an airplane and when he asked what I did (I was in my 1980s navy blue suit with mock tie), I proudly told him that I worked for the largest transit consulting firm in the world. His response was: "I can see that you are proud of that, but don't put too much stock in size. What would you think if I told you that I had married the largest woman in the world?"

≈

Small businesses represent 99.7 percent of all employer firms. They employ over half of the private sector employees, pay 44 percent of total U.S. payroll and have generated 64 percent of net new jobs over the past 15 years.[5] "Small businesses make up 97.3 percent of all identified exporters . . . and produce 13 times more patents per employee than large patenting firms. These patents are twice as likely as large firm patents to be among the one percent most cited."[6]

WHAT WE DO KNOW

"Between 6 percent and 7 percent of the U.S. population is in the process of starting a business at any given time.[7]

In 2010, an average of 565,000 new businesses were created each month.[8] Additionally, "Of the total labor force, more than 3.9 million people were "moonlighters" involved in both self-employment and wage-and-salary work.

"While only half of new firms survive to age five, 80 percent of the jobs created by the firm survive five years." [9]

The five primary reasons for failure are: lack of sufficient capital (by far the biggest reason), lack of focus, meager marketing, poor execution, and failure to recognize when "good enough" is "good enough" for the marketplace.[10]

THE INCREASING NUMBER OF WOMEN CONSULTANTS

A 1986 survey of women-owned businesses indicates that 7.6% of them were consulting practices.[11] The authors note that, despite their research efforts, they could not locate any more current or updated data regarding women-owned consulting practices than the 1986 study. Perhaps it's the myriad definitions of "consultant" that are causing the difficulty?

THE GROWTH IN SMALL BUSINESS OWNERSHIP AND ENTREPRENEURSHIP

"Entrepreneurs rightly command enormous respect, and their contributions to the U.S. economy are followed by academics and policymakers alike."[12]

While the president of the United States has been advised to consider the impact of entrepreneurs in the Small Business Administration Report to the President,[13] small business owners do not always consider themselves entrepreneurs.

Many of Terri's clients describe themselves as "just small business owners."

Originally, Terri tended to consider small business ownership and entrepreneurs in the same category. Now, she recognizes that while small businesses and entrepreneurial businesses have many of the same issues, they solve problems differently.

Now, Terri recognizes many divisions. Some firm owners are:

- Entrepreneurial founders and owners with a desire to start small and get big —these are sometimes called Gazelles.
- Small business owners who determine that a "Mom and Pop" operation is their desire. These business owners are sometimes referred to as Lifestyle Entrepreneurs—an individual who chooses small business ownership as a means to support her family and/or satisfy her own personal motivations.
- Some companies are Hybrids, usually companies in transition – originally companies designed to be small for lifestyle purposes, and then grown when the owner's lifestyle changes or the next generation assumes ownership.

For example, in 1981, in Cincinnati, Ohio, Candace Kendle began a small consulting business to spend more time with her children. Once her children were grown, she expanded the business into a leading pharmaceutical research firm, Kendle International (NASDAQ: KNDL) that is publicly traded, operates in eighty countries, and is recognized as one of Fortune's 100 Fastest Growing Companies in 2008. In May 2011, Kendle announced the sale of the business to a larger firm in her industry, INC Research, for $232 million; she remains as chairman of the company's board.

Regardless of the label: micro, mini, small or entrepreneurial (or Gazelle, Lifestyle, or Hybrid) – the smaller-than-500-employee firms have grown and continue to increase. Increasingly, women are the heads of these companies: "Far more than 50 percent of new businesses started in the U.S. are started by women." [14]

WHAT ELSE DO WE KNOW?

"There are about six million businesses in the United States that employ people other than the owners(s). Ninety percent of them employ fewer than 20 people. In addition, about 20 million people operate full- and part-time firms that do not employ others." [15]

"American small business is the world's second largest economy, trailing only the U.S. as a whole, but ahead of Japan, China and the U.K." [16]

This book's focus is the small consulting practice in the United States, more specifically in the Midwest. We do sparingly address small business ownership in other countries; the non-US statistics and observations indicate that the small business ownership wave is not unique to the United States, it is indeed worldwide.

Terri

In 1998, in an article under "Growth Strategies," published in the local business newspaper I discussed creating a work-family balance while my son was still in high school and limiting my practice to the regional area so that I did not have to travel overnight. I had become a primary parent to my son. In that article, I said that once I became successful, I wanted to help entrepreneurs in other countries, such as Russia, to get started.

As soon as the published article hit the newsstands, I received a call from the International Visitors Bureau asking if I would spend time with a woman from Russia who would be visiting within the month and wanted to learn more about small business ownership in the United States. My protests that I was still a beginning entrepreneur fell on deaf ears and soon I had agreed to do what I could.

We sat outside on a crisp sunny day, and made the best of the fact that she spoke only a little English and I spoke no Russian. Despite the language barrier, we found a way to communicate. I learned how difficult it is for anyone to establish a business in Russia. The Russian mafia was a fact of life in that year—I have no idea how it is today—and going from a partner in a CPA firm to being on her own required giving up a substantial part of her earnings just to stay in business. I could not advise her about this; I had no concept of what that must be like. I try to remember that day when the tax bills come due. At least I know in advance the cost of doing business in this country.

≈

While the real growth in net new jobs comes from small businesses – in the past fifteen years, small businesses have "generated 64 percent of net new jobs."[17] Both large and small firms are necessary to develop and maintain a strong economy.

BUT, WHAT ARE WE TO MAKE OF THE NUMBERS?

It is not likely that America's first female millionaire, Madam C. J. Walker—the daughter of former slaves who transformed herself from a farm laborer and laundress into one of the twentieth century's most successful, self-made women entrepreneurs—began her business with the expectation that she would achieve such income or status. As an African-American woman in Richmond, Virginia, who began a cosmetic firm with products developed in her kitchen and sold door-to-door, her goal may have more likely been putting food on the table for her family. However, we'll bet that she found the money to be a liberal reward for taking her innovation to the market.

Money is the lubricant of the economy, the oil that smooths the engine of the small business, but not the engine itself. Money is the necessary grease to continue operations.

Where Is the Money?

That is the question women ask when they want to start their own businesses – and often traditional banks, the SBA, and venture capitalists turn the other way. Instead of giving up, women say, "To heck with them (or something like that), I'll just do it myself." So, on a shoestring, with children frequently in tow, we mortgage our houses, or borrow from friends and family, or max out our credit cards, and do it anyway.

Many women don't deal well with being told "no" or that they cannot do something. That only creates more determination. Withhold the start-up lubricant of money and we start our own businesses anyway. When we become successful, we create our own "angel funds"—dollars that fund other women-owned businesses.[18] As we grow we want to see other women grow and find their passion and power, and we will help to make that happen (a portion of the profits from this book, for example, will go to existing nonprofits that fund women-owned businesses in the form of grants or micro-loans).

Thomas Friedman calls this the "co-efficient of flatness." He says, "The fewer natural resources your country or company has, the more you will dig inside yourself for innovations in order to survive." [19] Women have known this for years.

WHAT IS THE FUTURE OF WOMEN-OWNED BUSINESSES?

Women have always desired choices; today, we have an additional set of choices in the world of work—one that directly rewards our hard work and our need for the intangible benefits. These are the choices that lead to a higher quality of life.

The choices we make allow those of us who are foolhardy enough (or wise enough) to believe that we can make a difference not only for ourselves and our families, but also for other businesses. And once we are convinced that we can do that, well, corporate America will have a different set of problems—going from not wanting women in the top corporate offices (the glass ceiling), to not being able to locate the women to fill the jobs. These women will be running their own businesses—the way they see fit. This is happening on a small scale today and it will grow in the future.

- Thirty-nine percent of women who are re-entering the workforce plan to start their own business. [20] Another 5 percent plan to work on a freelance or consulting basis.
- A 2008 Yahoo! Survey found that, "Entrepreneurial interest is highest for women aged 45-54, with nearly 72 percent saying they had "thought about starting or started their own business."
- "Contrary to popularly held assumptions, the highest rate of entrepreneurial activity belongs to the 55-64 age group over the past decade. The 20-34 age bracket has the lowest." [21]
- The response to a 2011 Yahoo! Small Business and Ipsos OTX MediaCT survey reveals that 51 percent of respondents have either dreamed of starting their own business or have actually started a business.
- "About one in 10 adult Americans is currently taking identifiable steps to start a business." [22]
- More than 90 percent of adult Americans would either strongly approve or approve of their son or daughter starting a business.[23]

If the current percentages of women-owned businesses remain constant, then one-third of those firms will be women-owned. On the other hand, with women starting new businesses at twice the rate of men, we think that perhaps the percentage of women-owned businesses will increase.

Naysayers will tell women that only three percent of women-owned businesses generate over a million dollars in sales each year. What they generally don't say is that only 6 percent of all businesses generate over a million dollars in revenue each year.

Even an individual consultant can generate a million dollars a year. Alan Weiss, President of Summit Consulting Group, Inc., tells us how, step-by-step, in *Million Dollar Consulting.* And now there's a web site devoted exclusively to women who make or desire to make a million dollars a year. The web site is www.makemineamillion.com. [24] If that is what you want, then "go for it." Remember that bigger is not better, just bigger—anecdotal evidence suggests that women own the size of firm they want to own. We think you'll agree with our logic: if women business owners wanted to generate over a million dollars in sales each year, they would.

OUR ADVANTAGES AS WOMEN

Today we are learning that we must possess the necessary competitive skills to challenge ourselves, not others. Collaboration, connecting, consensus building, and caring are the management skills of the future. The attributes of connecting and collaborating level the playing field for future women business owners. Women are the great connectors and we innately know how to collaborate.

In his book, *The World is Flat,* Thomas Friedman describes the "feminization of management" as the more desired future state of management. The flat world in which we live only facilitates and plays into the traditional strengths of women—collaboration and connecting.[25] Add the tendency of women toward consensus building and caring, also recognized strengths of women, and you have the basis of the future of women-owned firms—a flatter world and an increased recognition by women of their own power and passion resulting in opportunity meeting nature.

This book is a strong demonstration of the feminine phenomenon.

In the traditional male work environment, we are competitors. In our world, we are collaborators. We have experiences to offer one another and we share similar values. For us, that is enough to want to share our experiences with one another and with you. And, for those women who are of a corporate competitiveness mindset, we hope you'll conclude, "Well, if she can do it, so can I."

If you suspect that we have a bias toward small business and entrepreneurship, you are correct. We stand accused and convicted. We both recognize, however, that entrepreneurship, small business ownership, or whatever you label it, is not for everyone. Nor is consulting, our industry marketplace. Therefore, we have designed and included in this book, an assessment of your potential to become a woman business owner. You'll read more about this later. You're welcome to complete it and to receive a free assessment of your own potential for happiness in the world of entrepreneurship.

The presence of a market and making a mint are not the only reasons that individuals start businesses. Frequently, the reasons for starting a business are more related to seeking freedom, not having a boss, and feeling less pressure, as we discuss elsewhere in this book. Making a living and making a mint are two different stories. The point is that both women and men do not always start businesses simply for the money. Sometimes, they start a business just to make a difference.

LESSONS LEARNED

As veteran small business owners, some facts especially ring true to both of us. We share again those that validate what we see every day.

1. "Contrary to popularly held assumptions, the highest rate of

entrepreneurial activity belonged to the 55-64 age group over the past decade. The 20-34 age bracket has the lowest." [26]"

2. More than half of the companies on the 2009 Fortune 500 list were launched during a recession or bear market, along with nearly half of the firms on the 2008 Inc. list of America's fastest-growing companies." [27]
3. Thirty percent of new firms are women-owned. [28]
4. The flat world in which we live only facilitates and plays into the traditional strengths of women—collaboration and connecting." [29]
5. The attributes of connecting and collaborating level the playing field for future women business owners. Women are the "great connectors" and we characteristically know how to collaborate.

SUMMARY

We intend to provide you with a look at the journey involved in running your own consulting firm. And, finally, to provide you with a tool that will help you to assess your aptitude for developing a woman-owned consulting practice, so that you can make a more informed decision.

3

To Be or Not To Be: That Is the Question

"Twenty years from now you will be more disappointed by the things you didn't do than by the ones you did do. So throw off the bowlines. Sail away from the safe harbor. Catch the trade winds in your sails. Explore. Dream. Discover."

—Mark Twain

IS CONSULTING FOR ME?

Perhaps you're considering taking a leap of faith for the freedom and adventure of consulting. If you are, pause a minute and consider both the advantages and disadvantages so you can make a reasoned decision. Linda has been a consultant for twenty years, and Terri for seventeen years. We have thoroughly enjoyed the challenges and rewards; however, we both thought long and hard before taking the leap. In this chapter, we'll cover the key questions we think must be addressed by women who are considering the consulting field.

WHAT IS CONSULTING?

Consulting Definition

Literally, consulting means "to take counsel, meet and consider".

In the twenty-first century, consulting is considered a professional service provided by experts. A consultant and a client work together to achieve an objective that is in the best interest of the client.

What Do Consultants Do?

Consultants work with clients to improve the client's situation.

THE CONSULTING PROCESS

The process of consulting involves understanding the complexity of a client's organization: structures, processes and products, as well as the uniqueness of the organization. Consulting involves understanding the situation, the presenting issue, the underlying dynamics and, if possible, the root cause of the problem. Consulting involves proposing useful plans, including options where possible. And, consulting involves presenting options that the client has the resources to implement, including timelines, milestones, and costs for implementation.

A Consulting Business

A consulting business involves providing expert advice and making enough money to satisfy our ultimate goal(s) through the firm.

Linda

Before a person can give "expert" advice, she must have experience and knowledge in her field. One of the worst mistakes I've observed new consultants make is taking on projects that are clearly not in their realm of expertise. As a consultant, you will be regarded as one who has "been there, done that" . . . often enough to have learned some lessons worth passing on. If you don't have substantive experience in an area, your credibility will take a nose dive once that fact is discovered by the client.

As Linda mentioned, becoming a consultant requires some level of expert status. In a Harvard Business Review article30 new research shows that expert status is achieved by at least a decade of deliberate practice—practice that focuses on tasks that reach beyond your current level of expertise, as well as locating a well-informed coach or coaches to guide you and teach you, and to help you learn to "coach" yourself.

"The development of genuine expertise requires struggle, sacrifice, and honest, often painful self-assessment. There are no shortcuts. It will take you at least a decade to achieve expertise, and you will need to invest that time wisely, by engaging in 'deliberate practice,' practice that focuses on tasks beyond your current level of competence and comfort. You will need a well-informed coach not only to guide you through deliberate practice, but also to help you learn how to coach yourself. . . . Two kinds of learning are involved: improving the skills you already have and extending the reach and range of your skills."[31]

The authors of "The Making of an Expert"[32] study examined a wide variety of areas including surgery, acting, chess, writing, computer programming, ballet, music, aviation, firefighting, and many others. Some highlights of that article are as follows:

- "Experts are made, not born."
- "Real experts seek out constructive, even painful feedback."
- "Very few experts are able to engage in more than four to five hours of high concentration and deliberate practice at a time. Most only set aside a couple of hours per day . . . "

The article goes on to point out that it takes time—roughly 7,000 to 10,000 hours of intense training to become an expert. Author Jeffery A. Timmons[33] has said that it takes 50,000 hunks and chunks of experience to become an expert (maybe 50,000 hunks and chunks are equal to 10,000 hours).

Clearly, experience is not a one-time project, program or experience. Neither is gaining perspective. The more areas of experience and viewpoints a consultant enjoys, the more valuable the consultant is to clients.

Amazingly, however, the article goes on to suggest that only two to four hours of deliberate practice a day is required. If we take two hours per day times 365 days per year, that would be 730 hours of work per year. Over the course of ten years, that may get you to expert status.

My husband began delivering newspapers fifteen hours a week when he was twelve years old. By the time he was seventeen, he had amassed 3,900 hours of distributing papers. Two years into his experience, he added collections to his job, with an additional fifteen hours each week for that activity. That resulted in gathering another 2,340 hours to his expertise. He added supervising other newspaper delivery people during the next two years, adding 728 hours of supervision each year. So two years of supervision added up to 1,456 hours. Now, he had 3,900 hours of deliveries, 2,340 hours of collections, and 1,456 hours of supervising time for a total of 7,696 hours of expertise.

Recently, I asked him if he thought he could have run a delivery service based on that 7,000 hours of experience. He said yes. Therefore, it seems to me that he had achieved expert status—deliberate practice of his base activity, plus activities beyond the scope of the original job—collections, then, supervision. Would he also be qualified to consult on "How to run a newspaper delivery service?"? Probably. At seventeen.

So, it is not the age of the individual, but the specific experience of the individual and constant practice and personal growth that creates expertise. Was he qualified to run a newspaper? No. Was he qualified to own and operate a newspaper delivery service? Yes.

Enthusiastic support by family during the developmental years is also a criterion under the Harvard authors' definition of expert. I have learned something important, however, through my association with the women at the Urban Learning Center[34]—individuals who miss out on parental or family support during their developmental years can become successful! In other words, missing out on that support in those tender, early years is not a disqualifier for success. A support network later in life can have the same impact. A support network doesn't have to be a "traditional" family. The support system can be a community of adults; in fact, the adult learners at the Urban Learning Center have been successful with the help of a community of peers and the support of the dedicated educational staff members and teachers.

nda

WHAT ISN'T CONSULTING?

I've probably talked more people out of going into consulting than coming into the field by telling them what consulting isn't. Consulting is not:

A sure fire way to get rich . . . quick;

An easy way to make a living;

Considered by one and all as a prestigious role in society; or

The best way to earn a living while in transition between jobs.

Established consultants have built a reputation within the community, based on their extensive knowledge and experience in a given area. In addition, successful consultants share their knowledge in a clear, understandable way, either through training or one-on-one sessions. Building a consulting business takes time, patience, and capital. Consulting is not throwing together some letterhead and business cards and waiting for people to call and ask for your help. There's a high level of competition for the services consultants offer, and if a person simply "hangs out a shingle," it could be a long wait.

SIZE AND GROWTH OF THE CONSULTING INDUSTRY

The United States is home base to the some of the world's largest management consulting firms, giants like Deloitte, Accenture, and Booz Allen Hamilton as well as many successful small- and medium-sized consulting operations, such as Point B, Censeo Consulting, Cliff Consulting and, of course, Just The Basics® and Gravett and Associates.

Market research firm, Plunkett Research, Ltd. estimated the global consulting industry revenues of $366 billion in 2011. This represents a projected growth from $345 billion in 2010.

Plunkett goes on to state:

> Consulting is a somewhat cyclical industry. After a decade of sizzling growth and enviable profits in the 1990s, the consulting business was forced to pull in its reins during 2001-2003 . . . . Consultancies posted significant growth from 2005-2007. However, 2008-2009 marked a challenging period throughout the world, in the light of the global economic slowdown and shrinking corporate budgets . . . with substantial drops in business during 2009, in many cases 5%-10%.
>
> However, as of late 2010 and into early 2011, corporate profits in general have grown dramatically, meaning that executives are more willing to authorize new consulting projects as long as they see the potential for a good return on the cost. [ii]

ii Plunkett Research, Ltd. www.plunkettresearch.com/consulting.

In 2009, the consulting market plummeted over 9 percent, according to Kennedy Research. However, despite positive year-over-year growth projected to 2013, Kennedy research shows "reason to temper consulting market optimism with caution."

We view this as an opportunity to get your feet wet in your new business and not as a deterrent to starting your own consultancy.

> According to the Kauffman Foundation, "more than half of the companies on the 2009 Fortune 500 list were launched during a recession or bear market, along with nearly half of the firms on the 2008 Inc. list of America's fastest-growing companies." [35]

WHEN DOES A CLIENT NEED A CONSULTANT?

Hiring a consultant is appropriate when you know something has to be done to resolve a situation and:

- You do not have the time to do it yourself,
- You do not have the skills to do it yourself, or
- You need an objective opinion about the situation.

Hiring a consultant is appropriate when an occasional, distinctive and/or technical issue arises in the business for which there is no internal skill, no time for the internal skills to be deployed to the issue, or when an outside opinion is sought to confirm or deny the root cause of the issue. In short, hiring a consultant is a good idea when time, talent, or perspective is needed.

THE VARIOUS ROLES OF CONSULTANTS

Consultants come in many shapes and sizes. Types of professional service experts include: accountants, architects, attorneys, business consultants, copywriters, dentists, engineers, funeral directors, physicians, recruiters, researchers, real estate brokers, and web designers, among many others.

Today in our field of human resource management, consultants fill a variety of roles in profit and nonprofit organizations. Some consultants choose to devote their practice solely to training, either in public or on-site seminars. Trainers can become certified in developed programs such as Zenger-Miller and Development Dimensions International, or develop unique or customized programs.

Other consultants choose to consult on a one-on-one basis with managers, sharing their expertise in specific areas such as compensation, benefits, protective labor laws, performance management or progressive discipline.

Yet another role is organizational consulting, in which the consultant facilitates planning and implementation of initiatives such as diversity or career development. The operative word here is *facilitates*. The consultant isn't doing . . . someone within the client organization is.

Another important role for consultants is executive coaching, to assist high level managers in their personal and professional growth. Sometimes it's lonely at the top, and executives need to share their concerns and solicit advice on personal development from an objective professional.

Outsourcing of special projects, such as writing employee handbooks is a growing area as well. Human resource departments in some organizations may be too small to devote a single person's time to a three-to-six-month project, and an external consultant can prove to be valuable in this instance.

Finally, consultants may choose to devote their efforts to conducting research, compiling and analyzing results for the client's review. For example, there's a growing role for consultants in the area of administering, compiling and analyzing results for employee opinion surveys.

The key is finding a comfort level with one or two of these roles and focusing on developing that expertise.[36] That's what we did, and you'll find out in later chapters why we're glad that's the path we chose.

ESSENTIAL RESPONSIBILITIES OF A CONSULTANT

The essential responsibilities of a consultant are:

- First, the consultant will do no harm to the client;
- Second, the consultant will understand the problem as presented, the underlying situation, and the business of the business;
- Third, the consultant will work with the client to construct options for addressing the issue;
- Fourth, the consultant will convince the client these options will ameliorate the problem; and
- Fifth, the consultant will persuade the client to make a commitment as well as the investment in resources to see the chosen option through implementation to completion.

Quickly apparent are the skills necessary to perform these responsibilities: experience, insight, and communication skills. Less apparent and equally important are the reputation, creativity, and ethics of the individual performing the work required.

TYPICAL CHARACTERISTICS OF CONSULTANTS

You may be wondering, "Do I have the 'right stuff' to be a consultant?" Consultants are a diverse group; however, we have observed similar traits across all successful consultants we have encountered.

- Ability to take calculated risks
- Self-efficacy
- Continuing education
- Self-discipline
- Marketing and sales skills
- Strategic ability
- Planning ability
- Ability to spot trends
- Comfortable spending time working alone
- Sensitivity to others
- Problem-solving skills
- Willingness to stay current

Calculated Risk

Because there's an element of *risk* in independent consulting, you should assess your comfort level with risk. You can (and should) plan ahead with a strategy for locating funding and marketing, for example, but a regular paycheck is not guaranteed by that planning process. You may write a business plan that shows how you will generate $100,000 in revenues in your first year, but your contingency plan should include how you will manage the business if $50,000 is your actual revenue. Otherwise, your bank line of credit may be in jeopardy when it comes time to renew the loan.

Self-efficacy

Self-efficacy means the confidence necessary to project yourself as winning an opportunity as well as the positive attitude necessary to bring about your dreams and aspirations—to take them from concept to reality. This takes self-belief, a solid plan and the ability to execute the plan.

Continuing Education

Life-long learning is clearly necessary to maintain your status as an expert in your field. However, in addition to your own area of expertise, you now have the opportunity to learn each client's industry, their domain, the company and generally some of their employees. The general business climate in your geographic area, the market, the economic projections, and new laws and regulations are all a part of your continuing education.

Self-discipline

Of all the characteristics, self-discipline may be the most important characteristic for consultants. Like most new consultants, in the first month of my consulting career I was delighted to discover the freedom of setting my own schedule. If I wanted, I could sleep until noon and putter around all day in my pajamas in my home office. I didn't succumb to that temptation. I set an in-office schedule, time for marketing, and time for visiting clients or potential clients. That self-discipline has served me well, for I feel I've been productive at the end of every week and still have the flexibility to do things outside of work. Discipline extends to work that goes beyond keeping up with the technical trends and making time for a balanced perspective through outside activities.

Marketing and Sales

The most successful consultants we know are not simply technically proficient. They also possess the discipline, ability and willingness to market their services. We're not talking about mass mailings to a list of names off a directory. We are referring to creating and seizing opportunities. Creative consultants use a variety of marketing techniques, such as networking, speaking engagements, volunteer activities, web presence, and teaching at a university level, to maintain a high level of visibility.

Strategic Ability

The ability to strategize is a highly prized asset—the ability to look at the whole, then to translate that into smaller bits of tactics tied to the client's goals and objectives.

Trend Watching

Once your strategy is in place, you will want to watch for trends—in the consulting field as well as the technical field in which you are consulting. We've found that successful consultants are willing to invest time in staying on top of technology and trends. Clients expect their consultants to advise them of impending changes that will impact their work and then assist them in preventing problems. Investing time in trend-watching and technology improvements is difficult, but the expert makes the time to keep ahead of new developments. To make that time, discipline is required.

Linda

Working Alone

Many consultants are outgoing and enjoy spending time with clients and colleagues, while some are more reserved or introverted. I'm definitely a member of the off-the-charts extroverted club! However, there are times when I need to spend time in my office, preparing proposals or designing workshops, all by myself. These time spans usually aren't more than one day at a time, but they could run into two or three days if I'm working on a large project. During these time frames, I have to be content with the company of my dog and be alright with quiet, reflective time. Of course I'm tempted to pick up the phone for a quick chat with a friend or my mom! I have to resist the urge, though, and focus.

Sensitivity to Others

You've no doubt heard all your life that intelligence, as measured by an IQ test is important to one's success. There are other types of intelligence as well. We encourage the development of another important dimension of intelligence, EI, or emotional intelligence. EI, or EQ as it is alternately labeled. EI has several dimensions, from self-awareness and understanding, to relating to other people, and from impulse control (such as anger management) to being able to "read a room" when you walk in to ascertain peoples' frame of mind. OK, here's a plug for one of my books—Using Your Emotional Intelligence to Develop Others. (2009, Palgrave and McMillan). This book covers the dimensions of EI/EQ in depth and provides concrete steps you can take to develop yourself in this area.

Planning Ability

Planning ability is an absolute requirement, both for your own practice and in order to serve your clients. Establishing objectives, setting a timeline and budget and keeping to both is a skill that takes practice, but one you need in your toolkit of skills.

Problem-Solving

Another key skill is problem-solving ability. We're not referring to the ability to react when there's a crisis, although that may be part of this skill. We're talking about the ability to identify the true problem rather than symptoms; the ability to creatively generate options; the judgment to select the most viable option for the situation; the discipline to execute the best solutions; and the courage to measure the results of your decision.

Keeping Current

Keeping up with everything that is going on in the business world, the consulting world, the human resource field is a full-time job and we already have full-time jobs fulfilling client needs and marketing our services. Nevertheless, we have to keep up in order to be effective and provide value to our clients.

SHOULD I BECOME A CONSULTANT?

"There is one thing stronger than all the armies in the world, and that is an idea whose time has come."

—Victor Hugo

At this point, you may be asking yourself if consulting is for you. Yes, consulting is a challenging, interesting, fast-paced career that can be extremely rewarding! But, first, ask yourself the following seven questions . . . and be willing to search deeply within yourself for the answers:

1. What expertise do I have that organizations might be willing to pay for?
2. Do I possess most of the characteristics mentioned in the previous section?
3. Am I willing and able to give up a predictable, steady income while I grow my business?
4. Would I prefer to be independent and run all aspects of a business, or would I rather join an established consulting firm?
5. Am I comfortable working on my own, with little interaction on a regular basis?
6. Am I willing to travel to develop my business?
7. What do I want from consulting that's missing in my position as a employee?

Once you have answered the above questions, you may want to take the self-assessment below. Once you have completed reading this book, you may want to take the same assessment a second time. You can view your score at www.justthebasics.com.

ASSESSMENT FOR WOMEN CONSULTANTS

For each item, place the most accurate response to the left of each number.

Rarely	Occasionally	Sometimes	Usually	Almost Always
1	2	3	4	5

_____1 I'm comfortable spending time on my own as opposed to working all day with others.

_____2 I enjoy brainstorming ideas with others.

_____3 I build relationships and networks of people to share with and learn from.

_____4 If I don't know the answer to a problem or issue, I don't hesitate to ask someone who's knowledgeable in that area.

_____5 When I do long-term planning I design concrete action steps to achieve my objectives.

_____6 To me, customer service is a way of doing things rather than a department.

_____7 The core values I hold are clear and strong in my mind.

_____8 I reflect on lessons learned from my failures.

_____9 I'm able to clearly articulate my ideas and opinions to others.

_____10 I view myself as a lifelong learner.

_____11 I ask questions to understand what motivates others.

_____12 I'm comfortable in either a leadership or team member role.

_____13 I represent what I believe to be my organization's brand in my actions and decisions.

_____14 I enjoy finding ways to capitalize on peoples' talents to achieve results.

_____15 I endeavor to teach through my actions.

_____16 I seek out diverse perspectives and backgrounds to enhance my knowledge.

_____17 I take time periodically to reflect on my future and my professional growth.

_____18 When I set goals, I also set specific success criteria so I know when I've succeeded.

_____19 People at work tend to come to me for help and guidance.

_____20 I have the ability to decide which situations to get involved in that are good for me.

_____21 I am sensitive to the moods and feelings of others.

_____22 I strive to keep my mind open so my assumptions don't control my actions.

_____23 I believe some problems have more than one answer.

_____24 I'm willing to take calculated financial risks.

_____25 I'm an empathetic listener.

_____26 If someone misunderstands something I've said, it's my responsibility to get the message across.

_____27 I will find another solution to a problem if my first approach doesn't work.

_____28 I have a clear sense of what my skills and talents are.

_____29 I'm confident in my own opinions.

_____30 People ask me to be their mentor.

_____31 I'm comfortable taking risks with my career.

_____32 Working with people who have different perspectives from my own is fun.

_____33 I can work in an environment that is not high tech.

_____34 I can accept change even if I'm not totally committed to the need for change.

_____35 I believe innovation is a necessary aspect of doing business in a global society.

_____36 I'm comfortable making sales calls based on referrals to promote my services.

_____37 I'm comfortable making "cold" sales calls on people I don't know to promote my services.

_____38 I have a knack for assessing where people are in their professional development.

_____39 When I delegate work, I get the results I expected.

_____40 I believe that I'm responsible for my success.

Scoring and Interpretation:

Score	Interpretation
> 100	Low probability of success as a consultant
101 – 149	Moderate chance of success as a consultant
150 – 200	High probability of happiness and success as a consultant

Visit www.justthebasics.com for a more detailed interpretation.

Here is our favorite recipe for women business owners (WBOs) as they begin their new venture.

Recipe for WBO Start-Up
One cup of willpower
One cup of persistence
One cup of intuition
One cup of discipline
One cup of connections
One cup of support
Add a dash of capital and stir.
Bake for thirty days to three years based on the heat of the oven.

WHERE IS THE MONEY?

Of the few sources of funds available to women entrepreneurs, self-funding is the most common, followed by credit cards, and friends and family, then bank loans (including lines of credit). The government provides free information and loans (not-free) through the Small Business Administration (www.sba.gov) Other sources of investment capital are: venture capitalists, angel funds and angel investors[37], incubators, accelerators, and seed firms. There are also micro-loans, which are very small amounts of money. For more information on angels, venture capitalists and incubators, see "How to Be an Angel" and Angel Investing.[38] Additionally, and perhaps unwittingly, many big businesses have funded start-ups through their layoff and severance packages.

The newest sources of funding are for-profit online social lending services. An alternative to bank loans, these services began as a method of funding small (micro) businesses in developing countries. The on-line lending services have expanded to meet the needs of individuals and small business owners with no or little collateral. These are also known as peer-to-peer lending sites that can be found on the internet.[39]

The old-fashioned way in the late 1970s was to approach the bank, as Terri did, with a business plan and this statement: "We already have one private investor; what we need from you is $20,000." Our "private investor" gave us $500 payable over five years with ten percent simple interest (but the bank didn't have to know that).

Recipe for WBO Success
One gallon of hard work
Substitute ingredients: Innovation can always be used as a substitute for missing resources.

HOW DO YOU KNOW?

Students and aspiring entrepreneurs often ask us, "How do you know when you are ready to start a business?"

My response is that you will know—when you have the education and the multitude of bits and bytes of experience that qualify you to offer something to others. My suspicion is that an individual has a defining moment, an Aha! experience that reveals an awareness that something is "not right" in her current employment situation, and she has gathered enough data to say "Now is the time." For me, it was like volcanic magma that the earth could not hold inside any longer – the energy and ideas and bits of information erupted in my world as though there were no choice.

Terri

The accumulation of those bits of information can begin quite early. My first little bit of information was a childhood message from my father. A small business owner himself (we called him a plumber), his business and I were the original playmates—we both came into this world the same year. If my Dad had more than three complaints in his life, I never heard them. However, his near daily refrain is embedded in my mind: "You just can't find good employees." He declined to teach his "girls" the business of plumbing, heating and air conditioning, but my response to his refrain was learning then sharing—giving small businesses the tools necessary to find and keep those good employees. Teaching small business owners the skills of recruiting and retaining employees became my passion. But, it took me twenty years of gathering those hunks and chunks of experience before I attempted to provide those services to small businesses as a consultant.

≈

From our conversations with young women entrepreneurs we've learned that flexibility, control over one's own destiny, and the challenge of leading a company are the primary reasons women in their twenties are starting their own companies. For the undergraduates in Terri's Entrepreneurship and Innovation classes, the goal is making money.

We've provided some reflections on the preparation phase for consulting, and now it's time to share the ups and downs of getting started in business and describe what can often be a roller coaster ride during the first five years.

4

Our Journeys—The First Five Years

"The journey of a thousand miles begins with the first step."
—Confucius

≈

The first five years can make or break a consultant. The challenges include:

- determining a philosophy around the type of work you will pursue;
- establishing a market niche;
- building a client base;
- staying solvent long enough to meet the first three challenges.

In this chapter, we'll share our individual approaches toward meeting these challenges and getting over the five-year hurdle. We've both been in business for over seventeen years, and those years have been replete with ups and downs, booms and lulls, good client choices and less than stellar moments.

THE FIRST FIVE YEARS OVERVIEW BY TERRI BONAR-STEWART

Terri

I find myself reluctant to write about the first five years, now that I am down to it. Somehow we push the negative back in our minds so as to forget—to keep ourselves positive for ourselves and our clients. Then and now, I talk to myself about remaining optimistic and use a few inspirational videos and quotes to maintain a positive attitude.

So, even if this is painful to share, I must give you the whole story or at least a balanced portrayal of the good, the bad and the amusing.[iii]

During the first full year of my business, getting used to an entirely new lifestyle was difficult, but doable. That year four major appliances quit: the refrigerator, the dryer, the washing machine and the dishwasher. There seemed no choice but to replace them. Well, I thought at least I won't have to replace them for another twenty years. Who knew at that time, I would be in that house less than three years? A subsequent divorce would lead to a quick sale of the house and, the appliances would stay in that house as condition of selling it quickly.

But back to the point, replacing appliances is not a big deal when you have a well-paying corporate job with a regular paycheck, but when you are not making money yet, and you have budgeted for a year's worth of expenses to get your business up and running to the point of making money, well . . . purchasing those multiple appliances represented quite a chunk of unbudgeted money.

Within two years, I had gone from walking into a store and purchasing the entire contents of a room: bed, mattress, box springs, matching dresser, curtains, coverlet, sheets, and shams, to realizing that only one month's expenses were left in the bank account. (It would get worse.)

That was the kind of difference it made in my life. Still, I loved the work, the challenge, and the clients.

---

iii Author's Note: Discussing this book with others while writing the book has lead me to believe that sharing our private thoughts in a public space may lead to creating smiles and laughter, creating bonds by that sharing, and potentially, even reducing the pain and suffering of others by letting them know they are not alone in their emotions.

HOW I GOT STARTED

(With some editing for length, the story that follows appeared in *Fortune*'s small business magazine in 2006.)

"I started my own business once I realized that I had missed the seventh year of my son's life. Realization and reality tend to have two different timeframes. My son was nine before I realized that I missed his seventh year. It still took a year after that before I actually started the business. This was no easy decision. I loved my job. I loved the company and I felt like I was making a difference.

When I recognized the time I was putting in on the job, I tried to reduce my hours to make it better. I was only somewhat successful. My relationship with my husband was declining and the stress was getting to me. Finally, I gave my three-month notice and planned a smooth exit with the president of the company. We announced my plans to leave only after the details of my departure, including my successor, were determined.

Three months after leaving the company, I started my own business. I had taken three months off to determine the next best course of action. I thought I would try my hand at full-time mom stuff. In those three months, I learned how to paint on clay pots, how to puff paint sweatshirts, how to make angels from craft scraps, how to weave a basket, how to coach soccer, and how to make flavored vinegars. I was pretty bored in the hours while my son was at school.

I knew that I would be happy only if I could have both meaningful work and the flexibility that I needed to attend to my child. So, I started my own business. It took one month to secure my first client and they got a real bargain. Since they were my only client, anything that was not sales time was theirs; which is to say, since I hated sales, they received all my time from 7 a.m. to 3:30 p.m. every day. That is when my son came home from school and that was my time with him.

Having my own business allowed me the flexibility—to help when my first husband's mother was diagnosed with cancer, when my father needed quickly to find an excellent retirement home, when my mother fell ill and died ten days later, to handle my mother's estate, to recover from a divorce, to (later on) fall in love again and plan a wedding, and to manage to live through the year while my son was in Iraq. That was the first ten years.

I love my job, I love my clients and I love my boss."

#

I live in a world of possibilities. That is my nature and also, by nature, I am an optimist. Working with entrepreneurs and non-profit organizations suits me perfectly. These individuals also live in the world of possibilities. I can easily see their vision; I can even expand on their vision. I like to make tangible the vision by creating a picture in their mind and mine of what that future looks like.

I am also a practical person. I like concepts, people, things, and data that are what the English call "useful." Therefore, I'm going to follow my natural inclination, and share a useful ideas or "applications" with you, like this one:

One client, when I asked about her dream, described to me a building that (with the parking lot), took up most of a city block and was ten times the size of her current operation. The mega-grocery store, named Thriftway that had formerly occupied that now-empty building became our motto. The employees picked up the motto and used it for inspiration. Deciding whether to purchase a piece of equipment or take on a new product line, she would ask if it fit with "Thriftway."

It was a sad day when a new occupant leased the Thriftway building. However, my client was a long way from being ready to expand to that size operation. Nevertheless, we still referred to it by "Thriftway" and used it as a picture of the future. By creating this focus, this vision that everyone can see, she will grow bigger and more focused for having had it. And, I fully expect her to operate out of that facility within ten years.

I began keeping a journal before starting my business in 1994. I was not consistent, but the journal imposes reality on the first five years' reflections. When we remember we tend to eliminate the negative and focus on the positive, but the journal reminds me that sometimes times were really tough. Therefore, as I share my journey with you, I will sometimes share with you the journal entries that I made. They are the truth as I saw it at the time.

THE START-UP YEAR

"When you follow your bliss doors will open where you would not have thought there would be doors; and where there wouldn't be a door for anyone else."
—Joseph Campbell

Dreams are the most powerful force in the universe. When we pursue our dreams, we become aware of new concepts, look at old ideas differently, and resources seem to appear where there were none. We begin paying attention to new ideas, new thoughts and new people because we have shifted our focus. When we share our dream—our new focus – and ask for what we want, the resources we need seem to fall at our feet. Then, it is our job to pick them up and to do something valuable with them.

There is a surprising amount of free and low-cost help available for start-up businesses, including resources from the Small Business Administration (SBA), the Service Corp of Retired Executives (SCORE) and many on-line resources. There are numerous books; I am an avid reader and get requests for the "best" books all the time, so I created and maintain a list. The books I recommend for start-up operations are listed in Appendix 1.

The Small Business Administration operates Small Business

Development Centers throughout the country and one of those centers may be available at your local university. I met the director at a chamber of commerce event, and got to know him through committee work at the chamber. Eventually, I became an official client of the center. (The SBDC gets performance points for enrolling clients, and he had the best performance of all the directors in the state.) There was no direct cost (the centers are funded through our taxes), but the "free" advice and counsel that I received was worth paying for.

The director referred what would become my first small business client (and this business is still one of my clients). When our community and I lost Sutton Landry at the much-too-young age of fifty-five in 2004, we lost a great friend.

Location

During that first year, I evaluated the location of my business by considering a free-standing building; a suite in a professional office building; an office in one of the "headquarters" buildings, where you rent an office, receptionist and conference rooms by the hour; and a home office. Based on the analysis that I am self-directed, not easily distracted, and an introvert who prefers to work with a lot of reflective time, I chose the home office alternative.

I recognized that by having a home office, to some I would project a traditional view of a woman who wasn't *really* working. Therefore, I took the substantial savings from not renting an office and joined a city club (think country club without the golf course). That way, I had a beautiful, elegant place to meet my clients, but did not have the expense of renting an office suite.

Interestingly, that city club, the Metropolitan Club, had less of an "old boys" feel than much of the surrounding community. I felt welcomed and relaxed. Since they were ahead of the curve in making women feel comfortable, now, seventeen years later they attract women members easily and there is a definite comfort in the fact that there are so many women members. The decision proved useful and effective.

Times have changed since 1994. The SBA reports that 52 percent of small businesses are now home-based. Nearly one-third of those were professional services businesses. [40]

Business Plan

I get just a bit obsessive when it comes to doing things right. I had a business plan, a marketing plan, a prepared presentation for the bank and a "dream book."

In the dream book, I put a picture of the car I would drive, the clothes I would wear, and a magazine cover with my picture on the front when I became a business success. On the cover of my binder, I added the following text from a friend and mentor, Nancy Conner:

WORK IS FUN WHEN . . .

1. You wake up in the morning and are excited about going to work—the anticipation.
2. You learn something new and feel that there is self-growth and self-expression.
3. The achievement factor is high—you win a lot.
4. The wins are recognized and rewarded.
5. Your co-workers care about you—you are not ignored.
6. You laugh with your co-workers.
7. The environment encourages risk-taking.
8. Communication channels are open – you understand what is being said to you and what you say is heard.
9. You are energized.
10. It makes a difference.
11. It is something you would do for free.

Here was where I was going. Wow, did it take longer than I imagined, but I feel great that the dreams have come true.

Today,

1. I wake up in the morning and I am excited to go to work—my clients are filled with passion about what they do, and it is contagious.
2. I learn something new every day.
3. I secure 90 percent+ of the potential clients I talk with.
4. My clients pay on time and sometimes send sticky notes with a thank you on them. Sometimes, they just call to say, "You were right."
5. My co-workers and I care about one another.
6. And, we laugh. I laugh a lot with my clients, too. (Sometimes we cry together.)
7. I encourage my own risk-taking. I take on client projects that are a stretch from what I have done before and I make certain that I do all the homework necessary to ensure my clients receive what they ask for and more.
8. I talk to myself. I debrief every session I hold with a client and ask myself if there is anything I could have done better. With established clients, I ask them that question as well.
9. I have a lot of energy. I give it to my clients and they give it back.
10. I get to see the difference I make in my clients' businesses.
11. If I were independently wealthy, I would still do some form of what I do now.

Today, I love the car I drive, I can afford the clothes I want to wear, and I no longer desire to be on the cover of a magazine—I would prefer to see my clients' pictures there.

Funding

The last corporate firm I worked for had a terrific year in 1994 and I earned a generous bonus for the year. That was the basis of funding my business. Savings and that bonus gave me the opportunity to plan for one year of expenses—living expenses and $20,000 in start-up costs for the business. I know I was fortunate to have this financial opportunity.

Banking

I did, however, visit my local bank branch manager, opened a business account, and shared my business concept with all the fervor of a new business owner. Becky Timberlake was encouraging and offered me a loan. I declined, but told Becky that I would be back. Every year, I went to see her to tell her how the business was going. When I made a deposit, if Becky was alone in her office, I would stop in and say hello. All the way along the way, Becky was with me.

Becky eventually became a private banker, a person who provides individual attention to wealthy individuals. We have stayed together. (I didn't think getting into this business that I would ever have a "private" banker.)

Image

I gave a great deal of thought, driven by my dream book, about what I wanted my business to "look like," including name selection, logo design, specially designed type fonts (don't do it), paper weight, engraved lettering (a waste of money), embossed fold-over cards (great for winning door prizes—all name recognition helps), and paper and ink color.

Equipment and Materials

I purchased a state-of-the-art computer, scanner and printer. I opened an account at the office supply store (my only business account, other than my bank account). My start-up fees were as follows:

Tax Accountant $1,500
Incorporation Fees........................500
Computer/Printer 5,400

Item	Cost
Fax	600
Copier	750
Software	400
Attorney Fees	500
Stationery Printing	2,000
Engraving and embossing	1,500
Identity package design	3,000
PR photo	250
Trademark Name	1,000
Brochure printing	850
Telephone equipment	110
Membership Fees—first year	340
City Club Initiation Fee	800
Database purchase	500
Total	$20,000

Today, of course, there would be a significant shift in costs, with hardware down in costs and service fees higher.

Two of my biggest mistakes in the first year, in terms of finances, were the cost of engraving my printing ($1,500, which no one ever noticed, by the way) and the purchase of Dun & Bradstreet databases at $500, which I had no plan to use effectively. Ten percent of the costs is a lot for start-up mistakes, but I learn quickly, so I didn't make the same mistake again. We don't learn by doing everything right the first time.

Three of the best choices I made in my first year were choosing a design firm to develop an identity package design, choosing experienced advisors, and the membership fees (for professional organizations and the city club).

Legal

I spent over two months in selecting the right attorney for my practice. I had a list of criteria including—small business expertise, employment and labor law, and female, among other things. I called friends for recommendations and generated a list of ten names. I narrowed it down to those attorneys mentioned numerous times and came up with three names. I called to interview them over the phone. I selected an attorney that I had worked with in the past in corporate America. All other things being equal among the three finalists, I knew her and respected her work.

Just a note about the legal structure of your business: I chose to become a corporation, not simply for the legal protection that it offered, but for image. I wanted the men in the business community to know that I was serious about this business. I believed, and justifiably so as it turned out, that they would take a corporation more seriously than a sole proprietorship. (You might be surprised at the questions I received as to whether I was a sole proprietor or president of a corporation.) A corporation, whether an S-corporation or a C-corporation, requires an investment in the construction of a legal entity, including attorney fees, corporate officers, annual meetings, etc. This type of legal entity is a separate "person" in the eyes of the law. A sole proprietorship, on the other hand, requires only that you state you are in business and file tax returns appropriately. As a sole proprietor, you maintain personal liability for the business and this type of business is a legal extension of you. You can find more information on business legal structures in Smart Start Your Business[41] or on the Small Business Administration web site, www.sba.com.

And, another legal step I took was registering my company name with the trademark office. It took eleven years to get it, but I now have a gold seal that allows me to use the symbol ® with my company's name.

Incorporation papers received, letterhead and business cards delivered, I was in business—or at least, I had a corporate shell without a client.

Advisors

I mentioned that I wanted a female attorney. That was because I made a list of all the individuals who would advise me in the business and decided that I wanted a mix of half men and half women. At that time, I had a preponderance of men. Eventually, I got the half and half mix that I wanted. The categories of those advisors were:

- Husband—male
- Financial Advisor—male
- Banker—female
- Attorney—female
- Accountant—female (first year—male)
- Best friend and mentor—female
- Professor and mentor—male
- Consultant and mentor—male

[Seventeen years later, the husband, the attorney and the accountant have changed; all others have remained the same.]

Mentor

Without my friend and mentor, Nancy Conner, I would not have made this journey of discovery—about entrepreneurship, about myself, about small businesses and non-profits, about my community. Nancy was instrumental in helping me start the business, in developing my first business plan and in keeping me focused during those first five years. Our regular contact was walking on Saturday mornings. The following story is drawn from a journal entry:

Saturday, March 15, 1995

I rubbed my sleepy eyes, glanced at the buzzing alarm clock desperately wanting to turn over and go back to sleep at 6 a.m. on a Saturday morning, but I hit the snooze button instead and closed my eyes. Ten minutes later when the alarm went off again, I jumped out of bed and put on three layers of clothes for my Saturday morning walk. As sleepy as I was from the wine and late hours of Friday evening activities, I needed to talk to Nancy. This was the only window of opportunity we both could find in our schedules—Saturday morning at the walking path at 7 a.m.. It was a half hour drive for both of us, and it was cold this morning. We would walk for an hour, have coffee at the local convenience mart and sometimes splurge on a donut—after all, we rationalized together, surely our metabolism was up and running by now.

Our walks became routine. The track was five miles long, so in the beginning, we walked for half an hour and turned around and walked back. Someday, we would get to the five-mile mark, but not today.

"What category?" Nancy asked.

"Let's do the short ones first today"

"How about children?" I replied. We both laughed. Nancy's boys were not at all short—they had exceeded her 5'6" height when each turned fourteen or fifteen; they were now all well over 6'.

It was ironic that Nancy and I both had the same sense of humor about things. We seemed so different otherwise. We really didn't have a great deal in common, so it was amazing that we became friends in the first place. The most significant thing we had in common was our love of business, and having our own businesses.

"OK, not much to report on that front . . . and she described the

three boys' activities, their wives/girlfriends/children. Nancy was a grandmother, while I was raising a teenage boy. (Of course, she started very early with her family and I started late. There was not that much difference our ages.) The other thing we had in common was that we just liked each other.

I took my turn and described the recent bicycle accident my son had experienced. I was raising a daredevil who knew no fear. In the hospital three times by the time he was fourteen, with near-misses more times than I could count. He had survived this week without the hospital, just scrapes and bruises—a lot like the real life of an entrepreneur. ("My son will make a good entrepreneur someday," I thought, but I doubted that he would follow my footsteps.)

On to parents as the second topic: everyone was well this week—as well as they could be given their individual conditions. No news here.

Community: Nancy was taking on a high profile board position with the local community college; continuing her presidency of a national professional organization; and raising money for the Red Cross campaign.

I asked Nancy about what community activities I should be involved in.

Nancy replied, "Choose three. One in your industry, one that is strictly business, and one that truly interests you—that furthers your own interests in a hobby or something you want to know more about. Look at who is on the board, who serves on which committees, and decide. Get in there and make a difference. Establish in the community the same reputation you had in corporate America. The community leaders will get to know you."

"Oh, and one more thing—make certain that only one of those

organizations is all-female or female-centered. You are creating a network of business people, not a network of women."

I reflected on Nancy's comments. Three – that would be hard to choose. I am interested in everything. My middle name had been "Why?" as a child, and I had never given up that curiosity. OK, I thought, I have to join the chamber—it is the most recognized business organization in the community. Which others? The local chapter of the Society for Human Resource Management. OK, that was two. I had to give that third one some thought. I eventually ended up with six, which was too many. I should have followed her advice and limited it to three. I do now.

The mile passed so quickly, as did all the other miles we walked and talked together over the years.

Thanks to Nancy, I got my first non-profit client. Someone called someone, who called Nancy, and Nancy knew it would be a good fit for me, so she referred them to me. When I made my first sales call on this warm lead, I heard a phrase that was music to my ears, "I didn't know there were people like you out there. This will be a good fit." They can't all be like this, I reflected. They weren't, but this one was.

I put my heart and soul into this assignment. I worked double the hours that I billed. I was pleased with the outcome and so was the client. (That client continued to be a client until they "graduated" three years later to hire their own full-time human resource manager. Many years later, we would work together again in a different capacity—but that is a different collaborative story.)

Interesting thing about mentors. You can't do without them. Self-made people are not really self-made; they had help. You know the phrase no man is an island—no woman is either. We need one another. I now mentor younger women to give back to those who follow.

Corporations appear to believe that if they assign a senior person to a junior person they have established a mentor relationship. I take issue with the assignment of mentors. If assigned, they are sponsors. If earned, they are mentors. Mentor/protégé relationships are mutually beneficial.

Another interesting thing about mentors is time. In a 2000 doctoral dissertation[42], Michael J. Posey stated: "Mentors are critical and must be willing to make at least a 5-year commitment to each mentee. Someone needs to walk them through the journey. Personal attention is key, and a mentor who operates from a strong spiritual framework can be of great benefit."

Reading Posey's work was an Aha! moment[iv] for me, as I flashed back to the most noteworthy mentors I had had in my career. All of the significant ones had made an investment of at least five years in my development. One of my early mentors was Edward A. Harvey, who, as I was to learn decades later, took a great deal of flak for promoting me early in my career.

Another noteworthy mentor is Alan Weiss, alternately referred to as "one of the most highly respected independent consultants in the country" (New York Post) or "űber consultant" and author, was kind enough to mentor me during the last years of my corporate life. If you read his pricing model, you will notice that Alan makes himself available to any corporate staff member as a part of his contract fee. But I quickly found that he wasn't going to waste his time and talent without testing me to determine the seriousness of my intent. Alan suggested that I read Albert Bandura's article, "Self-Efficacy Mechanism in Human Agency," thinking I would not.

iv See Chapter Fourteen for more information on Aha! Moments.

When Alan returned to town, I was prepared to discuss the article in detail. After asking me a couple of questions, he was satisfied that I had read and understood the article, and was genuinely interested in learning. Bandura had been a test of commitment. From that point forward, Alan was as serious about teaching me as I was about learning.

When I had been hired at that corporation, one of interviewers—a thirty-year HR veteran—had said to me, "You are not as smart as you think you are," and recommended me anyway.

Alan's greatest gift to me five years later was, "You are smarter than you think you are."

In many ways, they were both right.

And, the mentor who has been with me the longest, George Manning, professor, consultant, and author taught me the first and most labor-intensive course I took in undergraduate school. After that course from him in 1973, I took another and another until there were no courses left to take. Since that time, George has mentored me during both my corporate and consulting career. He has been profuse in his praise and gentle in his suggestions for my continued development. George has recommended employees to me. We have done train-the-trainer programs together. I have hired him to work in several organizations when I was the HR associate, manager, director and vice president. I have recommended him to my clients. George is a gentle soul with a kind heart. Without George and his guidance, I would not be who I am today. Mentoring relationships do not often last for over thirty-eight years, but this one has and I am a better person for this relationship. Is there any higher praise?

These individuals are some of the wonderful mentors that I had over the years. And, there are too many to mention them all.

I like to think that I gave back to the people who chose to mentor me.

In some cases, I was simply doing my job extraordinarily well, so that it was a positive reflection on my mentor boss. In some cases, it was referring business to a colleague who was my mentor. In all cases, I was aware that the person was providing me with information and guidance that would not otherwise be available to me, and that I "owed" them something for having done that. Each of them would deny that, I think. Each would say that I did not owe them anything. But, not giving back would be contrary to my own values.

Finding a mentor can just happen when you are doing a good job. Or, you can search for a mentor.

Mentoring is like networking—a two-way street and a long-term commitment. If someone wants me to become their mentor, they have to give consideration to the following:

- What do we mutually have to offer one another?
- How can I communicate, briefly and succinctly, my dream or long-term goal?
- How can I communicate, briefly and succinctly, what I want from her?
- Why would this person want to invest her time over a period of five years or more to help move me toward my dreams and goals?
- What do I know about myself that would make me a good protégé?

In Northern Kentucky, we have a program called Legacy, a young professionals group that is dedicated to cultivating future community leaders. They have a mentoring program that I have participated in for the past few years. This is a six-month commitment of our time to get to know one another. I have sponsored five individuals over the past few years. I keep touch with several of them. Only one however, do I consider to be a protégé. That person is the one that I will continue to counsel over the years.

Not all matches work. Like dating, both individuals have to be willing to try relationships—to make an initial investment of time and see where it takes you both.

Personal

During my first year in business, my mother-in-law was diagnosed with a terminal illness with complications that made treatment difficult. My mother-in-law was my second mother. I loved her dearly. She was a devout Christian who loved without thought. She also had little self-confidence outside the home, but over the thirty years that I knew her, she found her own voice, she found a job and she finally went to the hairdresser once a week as something she did just for her. We would go shopping and I would see something that she would really like. She still could not bring herself to buy things for herself, but then I could buy it for her.

It is difficult to describe what she meant to me. When her illness was diagnosed, she and my father-in-law (with health problems of his own) could not manage their new diets and medicines. I took two weeks off, went to live with them and set up menus and pill regimens so that they could remain independent. This was the role of the daughter-in-law and I was happy to do it. Therefore, for a year or so, whenever our son did not have a soccer game, we drove to Louisville for the weekend. I was back on the treadmill of event-to-event living.

Nevertheless, this and other family commitments meant that I could not give my full attention to building my practice. In 1998 when I went to my banker for a line of credit, she put down on my application that I had been working at the business only part-time for those first years. I had not thought of it that way, but I think she was right.

YEAR ONE—1995

"You gain strength, courage and confidence by every experience in which you really stop to look fear in the face. . .You must do the thing which you think you cannot do."
—Eleanor Roosevelt

My first year required becoming known in the community—becoming visible and developing a reputation for quality work. I had lived in that community most of my adult life, but I had worked so many hours and had been traveling so much I didn't develop a local network. I knew people well in England and the Netherlands, in Japan and Australia, in Mexico and in Canada, as well as throughout the United States, but I didn't want to travel and those contacts were not relevant in this new venture.

I decided to network. I volunteered for three chamber committees. I started, along with six other women, a local chapter of the National Association of Women Business Owners. I joined the local human resource association. This allowed me to get to know people and people to get to know me and the solid work I could do as a volunteer.

Six volunteer assignments when you have a significant amount of work to do is too many. I now limit myself to three. I am not sorry that I did what I did, but I would not recommend it.

In retrospect, my networking was successful, but my time could have been spent more effectively if I had been more targeted in my approach. During the week, my time commitment in the community was 50 percent; the other 50 percent went to my two clients.

YEAR TWO - 1996

"Nothing happens until somebody sells something."
—Mary Kay Ash

I was not going to be a successful consultant with only two clients. I worked on my elevator speech—you know, where you describe your business as though you were telling someone about your business in a short elevator ride. Seven words is ideal. You start by developing seven sentences and funnel your way down to seven words. "I solve small business human resource problems. And, you?"

I began giving presentations—free to any sponsored organization. My first presentation was terrible. I joined Toastmasters. Both my presentation skills and my confidence were built in less than a year. (I highly recommend Toastmasters for anyone who gives presentations. I learned more there than in four speech classes. The combination was terrific).

This was the first year of real growth for my firm. All the work before had been laying the foundation. I had managed by having two clients in the first year and four in the second. My savings would last until the first quarter of the third year. Now it was down to crunch time—I had to make enough money to live on as well as to continue to fund the business. Most people think that if you don't have rent and utilities and employee salaries that there are no expenses, but even with my little firm, there were expenses. There was $150 per month just in office supplies, $300 phone bills, plus membership fees and marketing and entertainment fees, professional fees and hardware and software purchases, etc. There were approximately $3,000 in costs just to maintain operations. Personal expenses and household expenses, like the mortgage, plus a whopping $1,000 per month health insurance premium, were on top of those expenses. Generating a steady stream of income to cover those expenses was a challenge in the beginning.

Additionally, these fixed expenses don't include extras, like when your computer stops working for no reason, or when you have a client who wants you to provide binders and copies of everything for a training program. This is when you get in touch with cash flow.

YEAR THREE —1997

"The way I see it, if you want the rainbow, you gotta put up with the rain."
—Dolly Parton

I became good at networking and was asked to share my expertise in a presentation to chamber members. That presentation was so successful that I gave the same presentation eleven times over the next three years. The room was overbooked every time after the first year. I was invited to conferences and gave the presentation to several in Ohio, Kentucky and Georgia. My presentation skills were improving immensely and I became comfortable at answering questions following the presentation—something I never thought I would enjoy, but now it is my favorite part of an event.

I was not so successful on the home front. My husband asked for a divorce. After twenty-three years of marriage, I was shocked. Our son was thirteen—the same age I had been when my parents divorced. Any psychologist will tell you that was "a compounding factor" in the depression I experienced.

My established clients stayed with me during this terrible time. I can't be certain but I think some of them pulled work forward to make certain that I had income during this time.

In December, my younger sister, Linda, called. Her husband had been in a terrible accident. I jumped on a plane and left for San Antonio. I was with her for the time he lay in a coma in the hospital. He never recovered consciousness. I felt so fortunate to be able to be with her. I stayed with her and her son until after the funeral.

We never understand why those we love are taken from us, no matter how strong our faith. While my brother-in-law Don was lying there, I had the sense that he was looking at the past and the future and evaluating whether he was going to return to Lin and their son, Brandon, or whether he could see an alternative future without him present in their lives. Lin whispered "I love you" and asked Don to squeeze her hand if he loved her and he did. While the doctors did not believe her, I did. He knew how much she loved him and he chose to go.

YEAR 4—1998

"When you get into a tight place and everything goes against you, till it seems as though you could not hang on a minute longer, never give up then, for it is just the place and time that the tide will turn."

—Harriet Beecher Stowe

Professionally

This was re-focus year. I was committed to making this business work, so I re-doubled my efforts for my current clients and getting new clients. Shared custody of our son provided me with big blocks of time on some weekends and I used them to further my business. I began to build templates to make my business more efficient; I increased my networking activities; I asked my current clients to recommend potential clients to me and or to provide testimonials, describing how I helped them improve their operations. I used these testimonials in the sales calls I made to prospects.

The focus paid off. I increased my client base significantly that year.

In November, my sister Lin moved home to Northern Kentucky from San Antonio. She came to work for me to help me build the business. She handled the administrative tasks, which freed me to work on the new clients. She got three years of the business organized. She also happens to be a marketing expert and developed the materials that would help me move forward. I couldn't have done it without her. This was the first of two times that I needed inside help. My friends (my sister is my friend) seem to be there when I need them.

Personally

My son and I took a five-day vacation that year—the inexpensive kind. We jumped into my pick-up truck.[v] We were going to tour our home state—Kentucky. We drove and drove. We saw most of the state and many of the attractions. I am geographically challenged, but my son is not, so at fourteen he became my navigator. We stayed in state parks and we stretched our dollars as far as they would go. We rented a pontoon boat and the motor stopped in the middle of the Cumberland River—twice—and we had to be rescued. We still talk about that trip, and he learned a little of Kentucky history. He also learned that it doesn't cost a lot of money to have a great time.

In December of 1998, it had been twenty months since I even wanted to see a male person. I called an old friend to celebrate my birthday with me. His job prevented him from scheduling lunch, so he suggested dinner. I wondered if this had turned into a date, after all, it was on a Friday night. We met at 6:30 and I was home by 8:30, so I guessed it wasn't a date.

v Once, I closed the deal with a new client because I drove a manual pick-up truck– the owner said he knew that I must be honest to drive a pick-up truck.

YEAR 5—1999

"It's not the hours that you put into your work that counts,
it the work you put into your hours."
—Sam Ewing

≈

By the end of the fifth year of business, I had forty clients. Some one-time, one-project clients. But more often, they were long-term relationships. One client graduated (got large enough to hire a full-time HR person); one client moved to Singapore. I signed on two significant clients (larger small businesses) that year.

Because all my clients were referrals by friends or existing clients, I had a mix of nearly 50 percent small businesses and 50 percent nonprofit organizations, as a result of the first year of operations. Coincidently, half my client organizations were run by women and half by men. Also by coincidence, one-half were on one side of the river; the other half on the other side—two different states. (My business is located on the southern side of the Ohio River, with Ohio to the north and Kentucky to the south.)

My client count, while I retained 90 percent of my clients, was and would remain fairly consistent for the next five years. Because they were small organizations, sometimes for two to three years, they would not need my services, but they returned when they were ready for their next project. The longest time between the first project and the second would be ten years; another would be six.

My sister remained with me throughout 1999 and part-time after that. She thought I was doing her a favor by employing her while she sorted through things after the loss of her husband. I tried to convince her that I couldn't grow the business without her, which I truly meant. She was very instrumental in my growth that year. I took out a business loan for the first time that year—the business was not big enough to support two single-Mom families, but it was an investment in the future, professionally and personally.

My fifteen minutes of fame came that year. In February, 1999, I was quoted in the local business newspaper as stating that web recruiting now "accounts for 10 percent of all jobs filled in the United States." That set off a string of telephone calls to my office, first from President Clinton's Council on Economic Advisors asking me to confirm my statement, then a call from *Wired*, asking for permission to quote me. Subsequently, I was quoted around the world in numerous languages, about this 10 percent internet recruiting. My, how things have changed since 1999. The new entrants into the workforce now ask me how they can locate jobs "other than just the internet." Besides advising them that the majority of jobs are still filled from networking, I tell them about the "old days" when the newspaper, both local and community newspapers, used to have all the employment advertising and that it remains a source (much diminished) for jobs.

Personal

That year my son and I took another unusual vacation. We went with a close friend, a nun, to Jamaica—the place she grew up. The story is long and I will not tell it in its entirety here, but I will share just a snippet.

Terri

We stayed in a convent, on the outskirts of Kingston, behind locked gates, in a room with two beds, one dresser, no air-conditioning and lots of mosquitoes. We spent one day in a children's home run by the nuns, across Devil's Mountain in a secluded portion of fresh-air land. All 160 boys had been rescued from extremely abusive situations—to the point of losing body parts and any emotional stability. It was a pig farm and the boys learned to raise and slaughter pigs—an occupation they would be able to use later in life.

We visited downtown Kingston—where the housing was frequently one-room, tin-roofed shacks in 100-degree heat. We were threatened with rape, but the local shop owners (all women) surrounded the man and sent him packing, while my friend, my son and I got away. Downtown Kingston was poverty beyond anything my young son and I had ever seen.

We then went to Ocho Rios to an all-inclusive resort for the weekend. What a contrast in the extreme! Opulence and poverty in the same one-week period; and a trip that will stay with both of us forever.

≈

That one male non-date was an intriguing person and over the course of that short dinner we had in December, we learned that both of us were now single. He was intelligent, had a great sense of humor and was passionate about something (my three criteria) and classically handsome as a bonus. So, I invited him to dinner at my house in January and well, long story short, I fell in love.

I was giddy, I was glowing, I was just head-over-heels in love. At fifty, you don't expect to feel this way. He was kind and gentle; he was an introvert, like me. He could talk about anything and what he didn't know about, he was curious about. On the other hand, we spent a lot of time just "being" together without talking. I was cooking for him one night, and there was no conversation, just a comfortable silence. With my back to him as I watched over the stove burners, I could feel him looking at me. I just smiled. Not only was this love, but I really liked this guy.

SUMMARY

"One is happy as a result of one's own efforts, once one knows the necessary ingredients of happiness —simple tastes, a certain degree of courage, self-denial to a point, love of work, and above all, a clear conscience. Happiness is no vague dream, of that I now feel certain."

—George Sand

Professionally, during those first five years, my primary challenge was financial, especially in light of the divorce. I did not find it difficult to adjust my personal financial situation to a lower income level, in part I suspect because I always lived beneath my means for normal expenses and only when I had cash in hand, did I make major purchases. My secondary challenge was not knowing how to sell. I did know but I didn't know that I knew. I learned that selling is simply developing a relationship and sharing with people what you do for a living. Relationships take time to develop and I don't waste my time developing relationships with people I don't like. If you do develop relationships and people know what you do, they will call you when they need that service. They will also refer you to people with whom they have a relationship. After that, it is delivery with value.

There were issues of being female in a male-dominated community, but primarily I choose to ignore those issues and get on with my work. I found that small businesses and nonprofits generally like to work with women consultants. Since I had anticipated a bias, I dealt with it by the early incorporation, joining a city club, and by just being the best at what I did. I had dealt with worse in another industry early in my career and I was prepared. It is the hidden bias that is the most difficult, not the stated bias. If you have experienced it, you know what I mean. If you haven't—good.

The *balance* in my life was easier than in corporate America. I had much more control over my time. (People only *think* that when you rise to higher levels in the organization that you have more control—that is a false assumption). The balance was created not by working less, but by time shifting. Contrary to the TV commercials and as I learned personally in the first three years, you don't build a business by putting in part-time hours.

Raising a teenager, especially as a single parent, is no easy task for anyone. However, I felt fortunate to have a teenager who took his risks one step at a time and gave me time to breathe, or sometimes just gasp for air, before the next challenge.

At the chamber's annual meeting with over 1,000 people in attendance, we had just sat down to dinner when I received a message that I needed to call the police station in my community. It seems that my son, now fourteen, had decided to take the pick-up truck out for a drive. I learned from the police that he had run across someone's flower bed, he was fine, no one was hurt, and he did not wreck the truck (that time). The police officer was wonderful and gave my son a dose of responding to an authority figure that I could never have matched. It does take a community to raise children.

Risk taking and dealing with the consequences is a part of life. I didn't want to raise a boy tied to his mother's apron strings. Risk taking for me was just a part of being a parent. You don't always know whether or not you are doing the right thing. You just have to trust your gut and do the best you can. There is no text book. The following was my guide:

Risk	Reward
Consequences	Certainty

When you make a decision, you have to weigh the reward you will receive with the risk that you will take. Are you willing to accept the consequences of the risk you are about to take? You also have to determine the possibility or certainty of the consequences.

> As a young child, I had a doll nearly my own size that I would swing by her arm around the living room. One day, her arm fell off. My mother sewed it back together and told me not to do that anymore. She told me the consequences—if I did that and the arm fell off again, I would have to throw away the doll. That was the risk I took—to swing or not to swing. Such fun! If a child of not-quite-five can calculate, then I must have determined the odds were in my favor. Unfortunately, I was wrong. My doll's arm fell off again. Her polyurethane arms were filled with stuffing and it went flying all over the carpet. My mother made me pick up every last little piece of stuffing, and the doll and the arm, and literally walk it to the trash can, behind the peony bushes. I cried and cried, begging for one more chance. That day I learned that when my mother told me not to do something and I disobeyed her, that I was pretty certain of the consequences.

≈

There never was a third chance.

As a parent, I was not quite as good at this as my mother, but I did my best. This is what I said to my son every day: "Be safe. I love you." I still do.

This is all the parenting advice I have to offer: "Hug 'em and love 'em—enough to keep them safe, create roots, and grow wings. Then, let them go."

THE FIRST FIVE YEARS—HOW I GOT STARTED

I started my own business in late 1991 when I realized I was too independent to let someone else be "the boss of me." While I'm a team player, and thoroughly enjoy collaborating with others (hence this book with Terri), I have my limits! I was working as the court administrator for the Sixth Circuit Court of Appeals in Cincinnati, which was a dream job by most peoples' standards, and one I found fulfilling and rewarding for the first couple of years. Unfortunately, by the fifth year with the federal court, I was restless and bored, not to mention frustrated by the slow pace of bureaucracy.

At a conference during my last eighteen months at the court, I sat in a session led by a confident, engaging consultant named Ted. As I watched him lead the session, I thought, "I could do that. Actually, I would love to do that." I invited Ted for a drink that evening and pummeled him with questions. Bless his heart—he was very gracious and spent two hours sharing his impressions about the field of human resource consulting. Ted provided me with "the good, the bad, and the ugly" in the world of consulting. The very notion of a challenge that not everyone could or would take on, energized me to start laying the groundwork for an exit out of the courthouse and into a doctoral program and consulting.

When I first considered a consulting business, I didn't really have a firm idea of how I would present myself and what expertise I had that others might want. I had months of research to do and interviews to complete before I developed a solid idea of the risks and rewards, the competitive arena, and what I had to offer that people would actually pay to acquire. My background was a mixture of accounting and human resources management, and I knew with certainty that I did not want to do accounting. I also didn't want to confine myself strictly to HR-type assignments; so I began thinking about how I could help HR executives build their areas of expertise, how I could help position them as my strategic business partners. In 1990 and 1991, this was a pioneering idea!

After talking with a few well-established consultants, I knew conceptually that some challenges would include helping my husband and friends understand my new role, living without a steady paycheck, setting up and maintained a legal structure for my business, and building confidence in myself to provide advice that could have a serious impact on others' lives and businesses. Until I lived through each of these challenges, I had absolutely no clue how scary each one would be. (And yes, I'd do it all over again, without hesitation.)

YEAR 1—CHANGING THE CULTURE IN MY HOUSEHOLD TO FIT MY NEW ROLE

One of my biggest challenges the first year was training my husband and friends not to interrupt me while I was working in my home office. During the first week when I was happily ensconced behind my desk, I was often deep in thought or working on my computer when hubby would breeze in without so much as a moment's hesitation or knock on the door. (At that time, he was a sales rep with flexible hours.) After about the fifth interruption in one morning with him there just to "shoot the breeze," I expressed my objection. Here's how I phrased my point: "If you wouldn't come downtown to my office when I was there and interrupt me without calling first, don't do that because I'm only down the hall. Wait for a break, lunch, or after work hours." He took my point with only a minimum of pouting (lucky woman that I am).

Here's what might happen. Your friends who work in more structured jobs might call and ask you to pick up their children from day care or run an errand for them . . . since you don't have a "real job." This happened to me several times during my first month in business. I was offended and said so! I encourage you to resist the urge to say yes to this type of request. I've found that I need to be as much, or even more, disciplined in structuring my day as when I worked for someone else's company. You may have other friends who don't work outside the home and call you when little Johnny is down for a nap. It's a challenge, but resist the urge to drop what you're doing and lose those 30-plus minutes! If you could arrange to talk with them outside of work hours before becoming a consultant, you can continue on that path. (And you should.)

MY FIRST CLIENT

Some consultants choose to invest in direct marketing strategies to build a client base. Because I'm a teacher at heart, I elected to respond to calls to make conference presentations, to teach graduate-level courses at a local university, and to write books to gain visibility and credibility. I haven't ever sent cover letters and brochures "cold" or mounted a telephone campaign with targeted companies—I don't like the hard sales approach, and I cannot handle rejection. Some can and do, and they're very successful with this approach, especially if they have a name of a well-placed person in the company to contact.

My first client, Roberta, was actually a friend and colleague before I started my consulting practice. When she moved to Cincinnati, Roberta sought me out because I was the President of the local Society for Human Resource Management (SHRM) chapter. We hit it off right away; I helped her make friends and become acquainted with her adopted city; and we have had a great friendship over the years. When I told Roberta that I was planning to start a consulting practice, she said, "I want to be your first client." She was the director of HR for a large health care institution. I thought, "How nice . . . maybe that'll really happen." Roberta didn't forget. During my last week on the job, she called to set up an appointment on the Monday morning of my first week as a consultant. For the first several years I consulted, Roberta was a major client who referred me to many other clients. When she announced one day that she planned to leave her "real" job and become an independent consultant, I told her that I wanted her first consulting project to be with Gravett and Associates. It was. What goes around comes around!

YEARS 1 AND 2—FROM PRINCESS TO PAUPER

Well, maybe not quite a pauper. But like Terri, I went from having the discretionary income to buy anything from a new bedroom set to new china at the drop of a hat, to having to carefully consider how much I spent at the drug store on cotton balls and body soap in a given month. That was a hard pill to swallow when I was accustomed to wearing new clothes every season and having a new car every five years. My desire for independence and flexibility in my career far outweighed the need for what I determined were frills. On the other hand, I didn't plan to be scavenging for loose change to pay for a spur-of-the-moment lunch forever!

I found out early on that consulting is not a sure-fire way to get rich quick. It takes time to seek out and attract potential clients (no, they don't come in droves knocking on your front door the minute you announce that you're a consultant). Just because you write "payment expected within 30 days" into the contract doesn't mean the client can't come up with excuses like "we never received your invoice" to delay paying your statement. Because I was accustomed to receiving a paycheck every two weeks without fail, this was a tough adjustment.

To make a reasonable living as a consultant, I believe you need to be in it for the long haul. I'm comfortable financially now; however, there were some lean times on the way to this point. I was completing my Ph.D. in Industrial Psychology during my first three years of consulting (and I don't recommend this path), and I found myself standing in front of the ATM a week before tuition was due one quarter. I was contemplating borrowing a quarter's worth of tuition against my credit card so I wouldn't be forced to take a teaching assistantship in exchange for tuition. I ultimately decided to swallow my pride and take the assistantship . . . and ended up with two excellent long-term clients who were students in one of the classes I taught.

One way to minimize the financial risk of consulting is to join an established firm as a salaried consultant. This can provide you with an apprenticeship experience, as well as a steady income and benefit package. However, it usually means that you'll be required to travel at least 50 percent of the time, and I don't mean to Maui. Topeka and Toledo are more likely. I opted to stay independent.

ESTABLISHING AN APPROPRIATE LEGAL STRUCTURE

One of the first decisions I had to make as a fledgling consultant was about the legal structure most appropriate for my business at this stage of life and circumstances. The primary choices included a sole proprietorship, partnership (LLC), and incorporation. I strongly encourage you to discuss these alternatives with your accountant or attorney before making a choice; however, here's a thumbnail sketch of what I found that each entails.

In a sole proprietorship (like mine was at the beginning), you get the blame or the glory—it's all on you. The control of the business, and the risk, are in your hands. Business liabilities are personal liabilities.

Another choice is to form a limited liability corporation, or LLC, which I did for my second business, e-HResources.com, and eventually what I did for my first company. An advantage of an LLC is obvious: limited personal liability for business obligations. Even if the business fails, creditors cannot attach the members' personal property, unless there's a case of intentional fraud.

The most common business structure is a corporation. If you decide to do incorporate your business, all we can say is: get a good accountant because there's lots of paperwork involved! You'll need to have an attorney draw up articles of incorporation, bylaws, and any number of documents related to the business, like operating or license agreements, depending on your business.

There are two types of incorporation available: S corporation and C corporation, both with advantages and disadvantages. We recommend you invest at least an hour with an attorney before making a decision.

Another big question is who are going to be the individuals you select to become shareholders of your company. The owner and shareholders may be paid on a salary basis, just like in an LLC. The corporation and the owner pay taxes. The company pays taxes on profits after overhead costs, such as salaries, rent, utilities, and all those necessary expenses.

YEAR 3—I COMPLETED MY PH.D.—WHAT A RELIEF!

Right in the middle of my third year of business, I successfully defended my dissertation and earned my Ph.D. I don't say this cavalierly because this was a very stressful time in my life, and therefore, my husband's life. For any of you who have gone through grad school, you know how challenging the preparation for a dissertation defense can be. It's completely consuming. One is not expected to have a life outside the academic arena. But, I did.

By the third year, my client base was expanding and I was heavily involved with my professional association, SHRM. I was state director for the association, and that meant meeting planning, conference planning, and endless follow-up on projects under way by several committees. Looking back at all the activities I was involved with, my immediate thought is that I must've taken crazy pills. Because that was crazy! I was enjoying the excitement of a busy lifestyle; however, I know that I neglected my family life. I left my husband, Ron, home alone way too many weekends. I was flying to meetings for the professional association or driving to meetings with clients or holed up in my office cranking out research reports. I've estimated that I had about a half hour a day with Ron. I didn't see my mom, siblings or nieces and nephews except at Christmas or maybe once during the summer.

I remember Ron knocking on my office door on Christmas Eve 1994, reminding me that we had to leave to drive to my mom's for our traditional dinner and gift opening. I cursed to myself as I was printing out spreadsheets. I really wanted to have that precious six hours to finish a chapter of the dissertation. I really wanted to be able to defend by the spring of 1995, and the pressure was on to stay on task and keep moving. Christmas holidays were getting in the way. (Have I mentioned that I lost my sense of priorities during this time?!)

CONSULTING OVER THE FIRST FEW YEARS—KEEPING MY SPIRIT UP DURING THE INEVITABLE LULLS

Throughout a consultant's career, but most especially in the first few years, there are times when business is slow. These sluggish times may have nothing to do with you and everything to do with factors like the economy, slow times for clients, or a myriad of other reasons. I use these times to recharge my batteries, plan ahead, and remember the times I've been able to assist clients along the way.

I use slow times to focus on writing. These times get me into trouble because that's when I typically decide to write another book! Sometimes I use these breathers to consider getting a certification in an area that would help me add a different type of expertise. If there are potential client companies in my geographic area that I've been meaning to research online, I start researching. I use the lulls productively to keep up my energy level and enthusiasm, and to continue to grow my knowledge in human resource management.

When I'm feeling down because of slow times or rough patches with difficult clients (which isn't often; however, it does happen) I pull out my "thank-you basket" from the closet. This is a wicker basket full of thank-you notes and commendations from clients and colleagues over the years. After five minutes of soaking up the heartfelt thanks and kind words of appreciation, I can't help but feel better about myself and consulting life in general.

Terri

I found it surprising to learn about Linda's thank-you basket; I thought I was the only one who did such things. My favorite aunt as a child was my mother's oldest sister, my Aunt Edna. When I was young, she gave me lots of gifts. No, not gifts wrapped in pretty paper, but gifts of love and ideas. Unconditional love was the biggest gift of all. I remember only two material things. One she left to me when she died—a precious glass bowl with ribbons carved on the sides. The other while she lived—a small empty wooden box. She said it was my "Hopeless Box" and I was meant to put things in that box that made me happy. Then, on a day when I thought everything was hopeless, I was to look into that box and feel the joy of better times.

When I started Just The Basics®, I decided to keep up that practice and put all my thank-you notes into one file folder. When I was having a bad day and thinking I had never made an impact on the world, I would look in my "box", see that my work actually made a difference in someone's life, even for a few minutes, and I felt grateful again. That file folder is larger now. I still use it.

nda

Before we close this section, I want to share a decision I made within the first five years that was one of my best. I established a personal advisory board for this phase of my life and career. Here's an article I recently wrote for a professional association newsletter that explains why, and how, I did this.

Creating a Personal Advisory Board
Linda S. Gravett, Ph.D., SPHR

As Human Resource professionals, we often find ourselves in the position of advising others in their careers. Our unofficial job titles include counselor, parent, cheerleader, and seeker of truth. We're busy doing this for others, but who is doing this for us? That's where a Personal Advisory Board is helpful.

Why Have a Personal Advisory Board?

Each of us has unique competencies and talents that we summon up during our career to move us forward and contribute to professional and volunteer organizations. Most of us, however, have at least one or two areas in which our expertise and experience isn't as rich as we would like. This is the reason for creating a Personal Advisory Board, so that we can round out our competencies and learn from advisors during the course of our career. The relationship that's built with well-selected personal advisors can be very fulfilling: a gift that gives back all of our lives.

When Should I Establish a Personal Advisory Board?

I recommend that you create a Personal Advisory Board now; it's not too soon. I developed my first group of advisors when I was 22, fresh out of undergraduate school, and transplanted to a supervisory position on an Air Force base in Japan. As a supervisor from a different culture and age group than most of my native Japanese staff, I needed guidance on being a woman—and a young one at that—supervising mostly men in a culture that did not support women working outside the home. My advisory board consisted of a Japanese neighbor, a man who had just retired from working for an American company in Japan; a female ex-pat working for an American company in Japan; and a person in my field at the time (accounting) who worked in the same organization as myself. This team moved me along as a work-in-progress and kept me calm as I navigated a new world of work.

I believe that you'll want different skills and talents represented on your Personal Advisory Board over the years. Have an eye to the future in terms of how you want your life to unfold, personally, spiritually, and in your career. Look around you (further than your back yard) and learn who has "been there, done that" . . . a person from whom you can learn. I've found, by the way, that my advisors are often younger than myself these days. They may have fewer years on the planet, but they have rich life experiences that inform my life.

Who Should I Invite to Participate on My Advisory Board?

For my advisors, I want people who will be brutally honest and straightforward with me, whether I'm asking about investments or adding a professional certification. That means that I don't usually ask close friends to be on my Personal Advisory Board, although my advisors may evolve into friends over time. I look for skills and competencies I lack, to serve as a complement to my experiences and perspectives. Over the years, many Greater Cincinnati Human Resource Association members have been on my Personal Advisory Board, and I appreciate them all.

Setting Expectations

So that the experience is positive and productive for both yourself and your advisors, I recommend that you set expectations up front, as you ask individuals to join your Personal Advisory Board. Be prepared to answer questions such as:

1. How much time do you expect me to devote to being an advisor?
2. What kind of help are you looking for from me?
3. How long do you want me to be on your Personal Advisory Board?

A Personal Advisory Board is not typically compensated by salary. However, there are creative ways you can compensate advisors. I refer my advisors to paying clients if they are consultants or have a product to sell. I offer my consulting services for free in exchange for their assistance. I bake them cookies!

How Often Should a Personal Advisory Board Meet?

I recommend that you meet three times a year, for one to two hours, as a group. Bringing everyone together creates a synergy and produces brainstorming that can leave you energized and motivated to move forward. I also meet with individual advisors, by phone or in person, once a month to touch base, and I seek out their counsel prior to making a major personal or professional decision. Of course, I pay for the lunch or dinner or have the meetings at my home and serve a meal.

Whether you're at the Vice President level or just entering the Human Resources field, I believe an advisory board could benefit you.

You may decide you don't want an entire Board, however you may decide you'd like a mentor or two along the way. Terri and I have both been asked to serve as mentors over the years; it's a role we've usually enjoyed; and we've certainly learned from in every case. We want to take a moment to share some thoughts about how you might find a mentor, either at the beginning of your consulting career or at different junctures where it makes sense to have some sage advice.

My mentors have not always been women, and my mentors have not always been older than me. I encourage you to think in terms of what you need to learn from another person, not the package that the knowledge comes in. My technology mentor was Robin Throckmorton, the co-author of my second book on generational differences. She's nineteen years younger than me, and I couldn't care less. I wanted what's inside her head—knowledge about creating and using computer programs that help me in my work. We did a trade, actually. Robin wanted to learn about starting a consulting business, so we made time to meet periodically to exchange thoughts on both subjects: using computers effectively and building a consulting practice. Now, I'm comfortable with computer technology to the point where I even became certified this year in developing and teaching online courses. Robin is the owner of a successful HR consulting practice. I'd say that was an even trade.

You can find mentors by keeping your eyes open and paying attention to people who seem to know something you'd like to learn or who have experience in an area you don't. These people may be in your current workplace. They may be a presenter for a workshop you've attended. They may be authors of an article or a book you enjoyed. They may be your neighbor or someone at your church. How do you know if the person you have in mind will be your mentor? Ask. You may be surprised at how often the answer will be yes.

Before you ask someone to be your mentor, though, I hope you'll think about your expectations of this person, as well as what you will do in return for the assistance. When I've been a mentor, I've asked for people to promise to serve as a mentor for another person within the next five years.

One more point —don't expect to call your mentor at 1 a.m. in the morning because you're having a personal crisis or having difficulty finishing a proposal. Establish boundaries from the start about frequency of discussions, length of discussions, and mutually convenient locations of in-person meetings.

5

What We learned From Men

Linda

Men have been entrepreneurs longer than women, so it stands to reason that we should learn from them. We're not suggesting that women in business should aspire to being mini-men. It simply means that we should learn from one another's experiences, and men have a different perspective than women do and can teach us some valuable lessons. Here are some that we've learned over the years.

LESSON NUMBER 1: KNOW WHAT YOU WANT

We've observed too many women who enter into a negotiation for a contract, a consulting partnership, or a business loan without having a clear understanding of their success criteria. We've noticed that most men tend to be very specific and firm about what they want. If you don't know what success looks like, it'll be difficult to determine when you've arrived. Do you expect a 25 percent commission on client referrals? Let other consultants know up front that this is your referral fee. Do you plan, based on appropriate market research, to charge $200 an hour? Put that rate in your informational leave-behind for potential clients. Be clear on what you expect before you enter into each and every business-related conversation. That leads us to the next lesson . . .

LESSON NUMBER 2: SPEAK UP FOR YOURSELF

Once you've decided what you want, don't expect someone else to intuit your expectations or treat them seriously if you don't assertively state your case. Speak up for yourself. We've observed that many men often place their agenda on the table in discussions early on, and they continue to reinforce their case with facts, data, and experience. That's an excellent lesson for us to learn. If you have a soft voice, practice projecting without yelling. There are also excellent speech and communication courses at local colleges or organizations like Toastmasters that could provide some insights into this skill. Let's go on to Lesson Number 3 . . .

LESSON NUMBER 3: DON'T WHINE

There's a difference between making your point by letting others know where you stand and coming across as a whiner. Here's an example of what I mean: I have an acquaintance who's a marketing executive. Over coffee one morning, this woman was complaining about how her male counterparts would go off to lunch or play golf and discuss mutual cases—without her. When she would discover this, usually through a conversation several days later, she would tell the men how her feelings were hurt that they excluded her. They always said, "Sorry", but continued to do the same thing. I suggested a different tactic: let the men know how they missed out on critical knowledge or information she had that would help them look good in front of their clients (or potential clients). When they realized they needed her expertise and experience, they naturally gravitated toward including her in their conversations. If she had continued to whine, they would go out of their way to exclude her. My colleague tried this new approach—and it worked!

LESSON NUMBER 4: CAREFUL NOT TO GET TOO PERSONAL

Most women have been reared to be nurturers and to be sensitive to others' feelings and needs. That's not a bad trait in and of itself. I've observed that men don't generally cross the boundary of asking questions that are really personal, while women may move in that direction. If someone who reports to you directly is clearly unhappy, it's certainly okay to say something like, "Is there something I can help with?" You may end up referring the employee to an Employee Assistance Program or a counselor. You don't have to act like the counselor if the employee opens up with, "My husband is cheating on me with another man!" You can be sympathetic and provide resources—you don't have to jump into their personal lives.

Here's a "take" on this lesson from Terri . . .

My experience is a bit different from Linda's. I work with small business owners whose business, personal, and community roles are so tightly intertwined that they sometimes don't realize when they are talking about one or the other. This is especially true of family-owned businesses where up to three generations are frequently involved. I have been through divorces, re-marriages, buy-outs of parental ownership, integration of daughters into the business, and trusted "best-friend" embezzlements.

Linda's point is well-taken, though. The most important reality check for me is to ask myself (always) "who is the client?" and sometimes in family-owned businesses, it is not that easy to tell. When a parent brings me in to help their adult offspring run the business more effectively, who is the client? The business? The parent? The adult child? Like most other situations, you have to ask questions outright and not assume.

The next most important thing is to remain in your "adult" state of mind when dealing with the client. You cannot become a part of the problem by getting so involved that you are no longer objective. Within those guidelines of objectivity and understanding who the client is, you will be able to be empathetic at the same time you offer your professional advice from an objective perspective.

Terri

LESSON NUMBER 5: LISTEN TO THE ADVICE THAT MEN HAVE TO OFFER

Listening to men's advice on business is good business—taking their advice is up to you. Early in my career, one of the men that I had was having difficulty finding common ground with said to me (completely out of the blue), "You need to carry a briefcase." In my blue suit with ribbon tie, I was so practical that if I didn't need a briefcase, I wasn't going to carry one. In fact, I couldn't afford one. But months later, I graduated from college, and my mother gave me a briefcase for graduation. I carried it for years —every day that I worked for that company. After I took his advice, he then advised, "You need a credenza." My office was not large enough to accommodate a credenza, but he sent one of the men to the storage room and found a small table (tiny, really—my briefcase hung over the edges) and put it behind my desk to serve as a credenza, of sorts. He could tell that I was listening to his advice so it wasn't long before he authorized an office for me that was large enough to hold a larger (used) desk, a used credenza (with my briefcase clearly visible), and two visitors' chairs.

The leather briefcase was heavy, even with just my lunch inside, but

I was in a male-dominated industry; they gave out tie clips at the annual industry meeting as token of the conference. That was the mid-seventies and a man of some importance and experience was taking an interest in me. When the general manager said, "My daughter has shoes just like those," (cute cork platform heels) I never wore them again.

In my consulting practice as well, men have been kind enough to offer advice. Without men, I would have only half of the information available. You get to decide, but listening is just being courteous—and you might just learn something valuable.

LESSON NUMBER 6: LOOK LIKE YOU BELONG

The former president of my bank once remarked to me, "If he can't afford at least one $500 suit, then he doesn't belong here." The poor guy couldn't afford a $500 suit (that's a $1000 suite in 2011 dollars), but he could have gotten a fresh haircut and maybe invested in a $150 suit, even if he had to borrow the money. I have done that. Twenty-some years ago, I borrowed $3,000 and went to a personal shopper and told her that I wanted to look like a vice president. When I made vice president nine months later, I am not sure who was happier—my personal shopper or me!

Most of my clients are manufacturers, or run small service and retail operations. They usually don't like to see me dressed up; it seems to make them feel uncomfortable. Some do, however, and then I wear my "corporate" attire, even with the client who always wears blue jeans but wants his advisors to look like Fortune 100 consultants. I want my clients to feel comfortable every time they meet with me. When I dress in more corporate attire, the more casually dressed of them usually say, "You must have a lot of appointments today." I suppose I have spoiled them. How delightful!

LESSON NUMBER 7: LEARN TO SHAKE HANDS AND MAKE EYE CONTACT

Men practice shaking hands so that they get it just right—firm, slightly upturned to the right, welcoming, with a message that declares, "I am here and I am welcoming you into my social space." My experience is that many women do not shake hands firmly enough to let the person know they are there. They don't welcome the other person into their social space. Instead many women stand just a bit too close—into the other individual's intimate body space. It's my opinion that most men see this as being too personal. Keeping the right amount of space may take some practice.

Likewise, making eye contact is good practice. However, if the eye contact is too long, men interpret this as one of two things: too personal or too challenging. The right amount of time is long enough to really see the person's face and put it in your memory to match the name, and no longer. Men are so good at this that they get confused when women "stare."

The list of concepts and practices that we have learned from men is too long to share in a chapter—it would take a whole book. However, we have decided on ten suggestions that we believe are the most valuable and common lessons.

TEN WAYS OF DEALING WITH AN OLD-BOYS' NETWORK

1. Be the best you can be at your job—become an expert in your field.
2. Embrace your uniqueness; know what you bring to the table and build on those strengths.
3. Find a mentor; once you have found her (or him), develop a long-term relationship.

4. Find your sense of humor; once you have found it, use it.
5. Develop team skills and build a healthy, useful team that achieves results.
6. Develop a network that includes both men and women and as much diversity as possible. Your network is the key to your future success. Your network, complete in its diversity, will form a rich tapestry that is about living a fuller life, not just about career advancement.
7. Make commitments and keep them—on time, on budget, with superior results.
8. Keep your balance.
9. Follow the platinum rule: treat others the way they want to be treated, not the way you want to be treated.
10. Be yourself—warts and all.

6

The Second Five Years

erri

A MINI PREFACE

My friends and colleagues include adjectives such as energetic, positive, talented, intuitive, and tenacious (another word for stubborn) when they describe me. I agree with them; I am those things and I portray those attributes most of the time. But like all humans, prone to the distress of multiple losses, I have sometimes lost my way and my energy and my focus. For those who want to learn what life as a consultant is all about, I am going to share with you what I call the tears years. The following words are born out of the discomfort of reliving these experiences, so that you have a more complete picture of a consultant as a whole person.

"Real success is finding your lifework in the work you love."

—David McCullough

THE TEARS YEARS

My business was successful simply by being in existence for five years, according to the standards of the Small Business Administration. Financially, 2000 was a very good year, and I continued to do good work for my clients. But, there were times during this half-decade that I didn't feel so successful—not as a business owner, but as an individual.

Prospects responded well to my passing the five-year mark—they thought I might be around for a while. While this generally goes unstated, it is a concern of employers. I know because for years I was the person hiring consultants.

So, I leveraged that success mark to increase my client base, and I maintained an average of forty clients over that second five-year period. About 50 percent were recurring clients; the remainder simple project or training activities. My focus was on building the small business and nonprofit client base with repeat clients. However, I also took assignments in which the client (often nonprofits and small associations) only needed help with one project or one training activity; I realized that these would not be on-going clients.

I did cut back a bit in early 2001 (from seventy hours a week to fifty-five) to spend some additional personal time in the first half of the year, I had a wedding to plan—mine. In June, the tears were tears of joy. I was a June bride with a real wedding in 2001. My dad, ill with Alzheimer's and missing all the cartilage in his knees, still walked me down the twenty-foot aisle. My mom was ecstatic to see me so happy and was there helping me with the final details. My sisters helped as well: Lin got me dressed, Darla took care of the pre-wedding mingling of the guests, Bonny sang at the reception. The reception and dinner were at the Metropolitan Club in downtown Cincinnati. One server, named Kathleen, became my daddy's personal attendant for the evening. The wedding and the reception were dreams come true. I became Terri Bonar-Stewart Williams. My new husband Tom and I jointly decided that was too much, so I left my professional name alone. My wonderful husband, Tom was, well . . . just wonderful. He still is!

In October of that year, I did my first live radio broadcast as a guest on Success Radio. That was fun, and while I can't tie any specific client to that experience, I know that was good for business. I learned that I could "do" radio; I also learned that people stop scanning radio stations when they hear people laugh.

My results on cable TV were not as positive; that time I was talking about community affairs. I didn't portray the same confidence. I would have to work on that. Besides learning that TV cameras did add ten pounds, there is the whole make-up, hair and wardrobe that is special for TV. Then, I learned that you need to learn to be succinct, pithy and quotable, just like you do for print. When you have an experienced interviewer who keeps to the subject at hand, that is one type of interview. When you have a local cable TV interviewer who gets into community issues, including personalities and the entire "who do you know?" question, then you have an entirely different interview. I learned that did not translate to keeping viewers interested in what you have to say just because you're enthusiastic. Therefore, the need for succinct and pithy responses. Let the interviewer ask the next question, rather than assume that you know what the interviewer or the audience wants. The interviewer is in control. Given that, I learned to be prepared in advance, with three major points that you want to make and be certain to get these points across in the time allowed.

YEAR 8—2002

In the spring, my new husband wasn't feeling well and I took him to the hospital. He had an aortic aneurism. At 10cm, you aren't expected to live. At 7cm, they operate. At 9cm, he was not getting out of the hospital until the aneurism or my husband was gone. In an unusual move for this hospital and for me, the doctor in the emergency room suggested we have a group prayer around Tom's bed (and the doctor said the prayer).

I lived at the hospital in the waiting rooms—moving from surgical to critical to intensive care waiting rooms, when they would not let me be by his side.

Then, my Dad was hospitalized with a stroke three counties away.

I ran back and forth from hospital to hospital, tears to tears, and prayer to prayer.

I am thankful that my husband recovered from that surgery and smiles at me every morning over coffee at the breakfast table.

However, more tears came again when Dad moved from the hospital to a retirement home. The traditional signs of dementia had set in and my sisters and I were unable to care for him safely in any of our homes.

The really tough decision to move Dad to a retirement home was not mine to make, but giving consent was expected. I worried about him driving, even though his wife, Nanci, tried to hide the keys. I worried about him walking down the steps without cartilage in his knees; I worried about the steps he had to climb at home. Mostly, I worried about not being able to stop a fall, or care for him 24 hours a day. Taking him home or moving him to one of the daughter's homes would be temporary at best. Fortunately, we all agreed that a single move was the best way—straight from the hospital to a retirement home.

My stepmother Nanci, had first choice of the times she would visit with him, and the four daughters made certain that Dad had company at least six days a week. Sunday was my Daddy Date Day, and every Sunday was filled with both joy and sorrow. I got time with my Dad all to myself, but he wasn't himself. Occasionally, he had moments of lucidity and laughter—but most of the time, he just tried to be charming and make conversation. He never lost his charm. For other visitors, he would fool them into believing that he knew them and that everything was fine. That must have taken so much energy!

For me, I knew that he didn't recognize me as his daughter—but he knew that I was someone who loved him. He greeted me, with a "Hello, Sweetie," and later with a big smile and "I thought you weren't coming today." If I went to the nurse's station and took too long, he would say, "I thought you weren't coming today." Sometimes he thought I was his sister Ruth and we were back in Colorado when he was in high school; I didn't try to tell him differently. I just told him that his brother Johnny and sisters, Ella Mae and Ruth, were doing well and that Mom and Pop were fine (even though his Mom and Pop passed away years before). He seemed to want the comfort that everyone was okay.

Many more tears flowed when I visited Dad on some days. He would cry sometimes when I was with him, but he didn't cry with my sisters. I don't know why he chose to cry with me, but whatever the reason, I was honored to be the one that he felt comfortable enough with to let tears run down that handsome, rugged face that I loved so much.

In November that year, my eighteen-year-old son announced he was joining the U.S. Army. He would begin his training in the spring of 2003. I cried.

YEAR 9—2003

"Nothing is permanent in this world, not even your troubles."
—Charlie Chaplin

In the spring, my son left for basic training. His passion had been wheeled vehicles since the earliest time he played with toys, so it was only natural that he went to Advanced Training to learn to drive a Humvee, then an Avenger. Then, he went off to Germany. All of that nearly broke my heart, but the worst was yet to come.

Tuesday, April 1, 2003

Dear Ashley,

You start basic training today and I will mail this letter as soon as I have your address. We will be gone this weekend to bring Grandma back from Florida to Florence. We leave Thursday night and will be traveling all day Saturday and maybe Sunday. I cannot remember if you are allowed to call home during basic.

Already, I miss you a lot. It feels like you have been gone a long time already. Everything here is so quiet. Your phone doesn't ring.

Do you want me to send you anything? Socks? (The ones you took were too small.) Peeps? (It's almost Easter).

I love you very much and I miss you.

You looked so surprised when I told you that when you are grown up that the rules change from being safe to taking calculated risks. (You know that does not apply to sex.) Just life decisions. You have the ability to plan and plan well. Did you know that it takes only twenty seconds sometimes to plan first, then do. The "doing" then will take one-half as long.

When you are in command, you will have to take time to plan, and then communicate the plan . . . then do, because people cannot follow you until they understand what you are doing. Like me, you sometimes assume that people know more than they do. I have to work on that, because common sense is not common anymore. People come from different backgrounds—different cultures and they do not always have the same "basics of understanding" that we call common sense.

When they understand, they will willingly follow you and begin to trust you. I have watched you plan and organize—in awe, for it is a skill that seems to come naturally to you, and that I have to work at. I have watched you organize thirteen people for an activity in fifteen minutes—watched you take three people and delegate what they are supposed to do—which phone calls to make—change priorities or times, and be finished in fifteen minutes. I know that you take such a skill for granted because it seems to come naturally to you, but it is an admirable skill, and one not to be taken lightly. Some people, like me, have to work at it. Some people can't do it at all. The more you do this, the better you become, because you trust your instincts—your intuition. You will make mistakes sometimes, but the Army has a process for that:

"What happened?"

"Why did it happen?"

"What can we do to keep it from happening again?"

We seem to learn best from mistakes, and because we are human, we will all make them. I have made more than my share. I like the way the Army focuses on what happened, not who did it, because that is focusing on the problem and not the person.

Your outstanding skills at assessing the situation, and especially the people involved, will stand you in good stead. Sometimes, you will not have time to plan, just act. When that time comes, you will know. Your skills plus your adrenaline will kick in, and you will do what you have to do.

Congratulations on the 6:15 mile; my best is 14:85.

You are so fortunate to meet people from all over the country! I hope that you will plan to keep in touch with those that you really like.

I love you very much and I miss you very much. I can't wait for your letters, so send lots! I will write again really soon!

Mom

Since Ashley would be gone, Tom had recovered and was back to work, Dad was safe in the retirement home, and Mom was doing fine, I undertook a fund-raising campaign to fund scholarships for inner-city adults to attend college classes in a safe environment, with lots of support. It was called the Urban Learning Center and I spend a great deal of time over the next two years leading this one million dollar fund-raising campaign.

Work continued. My speaking engagements expanded to regional conferences, where I was a luncheon speaker for the first time outside the tri-state area. The topic was "Networking Basics" for university development, marketing and alumni staff. Networking is one my favorite topics and most requested speaking engagement. I had my first experience in Atlanta, speaking in competition with the sharp clash of silverware on porcelain. Fortunately, I learned to speak correctly, from my diaphragm, so my voice carrying over the clamor was not a problem, but the distraction of so much noise was new to me. This is when intimate knowledge of the subject became truly important. If I hadn't been giving a presentation on a subject that I knew as well as the back of my hand, the commotion may have caused a disastrous experience. Fortunately, it did not and the program was a success (at least according to evaluation forms).

AUGUST 29, 2003

I closed the bathroom door and there lay his running shorts, tossed in the corner as he had jumped in the shower for the third time that day. I had just come from taking him to the airport for his big adventure in Europe, and my eyes misted as I realized again how much I would miss him. A year without him and I didn't let my mind wander to the place that knew he would face real danger. Instead, I shifted my mind's focus back to the running shorts and the big smile he flashed as he sauntered through the winding ropes of airport security.

The next day, the running shorts were still on the bathroom floor (my mother would be appalled). It was the Friday of Labor Day weekend; he had arrived safely in Frankfort, Germany. He called. The beer was "Great!" he said and the weather like autumn in Kentucky. "The air is fresh and smells like the leaves are falling." Still, the running shorts were on the floor and my heart was searching for a corner where it didn't hurt.

Saturday was better. The running shorts remained on the floor, but I could tell, reflecting on his voice in the two-minute call last evening, that this was an adventure for him. What more could a mother want for her son than Life As An Adventure? Hadn't I brought him up to see the world as both real and full of opportunity?

"See the World!" Wasn't that the phrase they used to entice him into the foreign-to-her world of the military? No, that was the Navy. "The Army of One" was the appropriate ad slogan. "Just a little individual with garments on his back." I still marveled that the little individual was now a nineteen year-old man with a big heart, a brave soul, and making the best of the Army life regimen.

"Let go," my mind cried out. "Hold on," my heart echoed back.

I reminded myself out loud "Every mother goes through this. I am not alone. Every mother . . . " and my thoughts trailed off. I was left with a hole in my heart and a patch made of pride.

In mid-October, my mother had an episode that appeared to be a stroke. Fortunately, her sister was with her at the time, called 911, and took her to the hospital. They couldn't find the problem—they suspected listeria meningitis, but the tests took ten days to mature. All the while, she lay in a coma.

On October 27, 2003, my mother succumbed to this rare disease. The tests came back the next day.

Dealing with a crisis is not difficult for me. As one of my colleagues used to tell me "I never see panic in your eyes." I don't panic—I just do. Just give me a crisis and I dive in and organize the situation, the people, and get done what needs to be done. And, thanks to my mother's teachings, I also assign work to other people. "It gives them a sense of purpose," she used to say.

As the oldest child, organizing people and events fell to me, and I welcomed it as a way to avoid the loss I was feeling. After the initial heartbreak of losing Mom, I went on to handle the estate. Now, I was feeling the pressure of having multiple jobs again—handling an estate, even one as well organized as my mother's, was extremely time-consuming. The fund-raising campaign was taking much more time than I had anticipated. And, of course, first and foremost, there were my clients.

One of my former colleagues, Vicky Rainey, became available for consulting work. She and I had worked together three different times in various organizations. While she sorted out what she wanted to do next, she agreed to come on board and help me with my business. She is a tremendous human resource professional and she was an absolute blessing. I don't think I could have managed to keep the business running without her. And, her caring demeanor was perfect for me and for my clients.

It seems to me that every time I need help, it appears in the most unusual way. And, out of unusual circumstances.

YEAR 10—2004

My son was deployed to Iraq. Fortunately the Army determined that the Avenger was unsafe—it kept falling over under its own top weight, so my son never drove one in Iraq. Instead, he became a member of the infantry. My heart fractured like the pieces of a puzzle, held together only by the thread of maternal will to remain strong for him.

Work proceeded well that year because I wanted to focus on anything except my son in Iraq, and since there was nothing I could do to keep him safe. Focusing on clients' problems was easy in comparison to where my thoughts went when I was unfocused. The more difficult the client problem, the better I liked it.

My cracked heart grew heavier as I realized I could not reach my son and keep him safe. He would now have to keep himself safe.

My husband just held me quietly when I cried. Some days I couldn't get enough of the news. Other days, I couldn't watch. I couldn't watch movies that had anything to do with any war —going back to the Romans. Flashbacks of the TV coverage of Vietnam loomed in my nightmares, when I could sleep.

Vicky Rainey remained with me through most of that year. When she was re-focused and decided on what she wanted, and I thought I was ready to handle the business again on my own, we parted once again. I can't help thinking there will be another time that we will work together.

SUMMARY

Without my family and friends, I wouldn't have made it through the second five years of my business. Secondarily, time-shifting took on a new meaning to me. Having my own business, with responsibility for only one employee, meant that I could work when I could work. I had to continue to work, to sell, to market, to deliver. The good part was that I got to choose when to do that work.

Corporate America can be understanding when executives are absent for family matters, but their time tolerance is short. "Take all the time you need" really means "take a few days off and take care of this so that you can get back to work." Maybe that is not true in every corporate culture, but given my orientation to work, that is how I interpreted that message (and, how I managed it from a HR perspective). Would that interpretation be different today? Yes. Unfortunately, it's experience that is the only teacher of value when dealing with human beings. As my Dad said so many times, "Walk a mile in the chief's moccasins before you judge him."

AT THE TEN-YEAR MARK

After ten years, I had forty clients, I served on three boards and one governor's commission. I taught a class in Innovation and Entrepreneurship at the local university. My alma mater named me one of their success stories. I led a campaign to raise a million dollars to allow inner city adults to go to college for the first time. My son joined the Army and survived a year in Iraq. His father and I divorced but remain friends. I married my soul mate.

It took nearly three years and a writing class to open the floodgates again, and for me to learn to grieve the loss of my mother. Three months later, my father died.

Those were the tears years.

da

THE NEXT 5 YEARS—I HAD SOME TEARS, TOO

At the beginning of my second five years of consulting, my mother-in-law, whom I loved very much, died unexpectedly of a heart attack. I was in Memphis working with a client when I checked my voice messages right before going into a training session at a hotel. The message was from a nurse at a Cincinnati hospital saying that they had tried to contact my husband and had my number as a back-up. The message was simply, "Please call the hospital at this number. It's about your mother-in-law, Margaret." When I immediately called the hospital, I discovered that my husband had since been located and heard the same news I was about to hear—my beloved mother-in-law was gone. I cancelled the training session and flew home immediately. It was a Tuesday.

I had received a call from my husband only the night before to tell me that our eleven-year-old dog had been diagnosed that day with cancer and had only days to live. I was feeling low because my business trip would take me through the end of the week, causing me to lose precious time with my "baby." I'm glad I was able to help my husband with funeral arrangements and be there when our dog was put to sleep. We grieved together, my husband and I, for both losses. It actually was a process that started to bring us closer together. We had seen very little of each other during the time I was starting my consulting business and finishing my

Ph.D. In a one-week time span, my eyes were opened to what was really important—my loved ones. It was a huge wake-up call for me. I think it saved my marriage.

My focus shifted from taking out-of-town assignments to pursuing area consulting projects. The fees were lower in my area; however, the travel was less. The decision was a no brainer—I continued my focus on jobs in the Greater Cincinnati area. I had been very active in my national professional association, the Society for Human Resource Management (SHRM), which meant a great deal of travel. I turned down the next offer for a high-level volunteer position that would've meant 10-plus hours of time away from my family each week. The result of this found time was that I began accepting projects through a local university, Xavier University. This decision resulted in an ongoing partnership that has lasted for fourteen years. Things really do have a way of working out the way they should. Over the years, I've had quite a few "opportunities" that seemed great at the time, and financially lucrative on the surface. However, experience has taught me—and I've learned—to dig deep and to take time to pause, and reflect on whether the projects were in tune with my personal values, before even taking the next step of exploring them seriously.

I have a strong need to serve as a mentor for younger professionals. Since I was in town for longer periods of time, I had the opportunity during my second five years to accept requests to mentor graduate students or brand-new consultants. I still do this today, and it gives me tremendous satisfaction—especially when my protégées become successful and end up teaching me!

During my second five years as a consultant, I had a milestone birthday: Fifty. I celebrated the entire year! My husband surprised me

with a gift that I wouldn't have imagined—The Richard Petty Driving Experience. Here's photo of me standing beside the race car I drove for eight laps around the Sparta Kentucky Speedway at 135 miles per hour!

My friends were amazed that I had the courage to get into such a car, let alone drive it by myself at such a speed. Actually, my experiences in starting my own business and traveling all over the world strengthened my courage over the years. Compared to some of the other experiences I had in life, this was pretty tame. I loved it—especially when I climbed out of the car and saw my grandchildren looking at me with admiration and awe!

My challenge to you as a reader is to ask yourself, "What do I have on my 'bucket list' that I keep dreaming about doing?" Whatever that is, please don't wait. Each moment is precious and you can't retrieve it. You can take a step each day to reach a goal that you hold dear—so that before you know it, that goal is both near and dear.

AT THE TEN-YEAR MARK

At my ten-year anniversary in 2001, I had thirty-seven clients, a dozen of which had been with me since the beginning. I was feeling like my life was in balance, with a stable marriage, a gorgeous grandson who was born in 1998, and work that was rewarding and stimulating. All things considered, life was pretty darn good, and I was thankful for all of it.

In planning for years 2001-2006, I decided to focus on two leading-edge topics for my consulting business—generational differences and emotional intelligence. These are two areas that personally interested me, and I thought it would be helpful to my clients to advance my knowledge in these areas. I'm so glad I went in this direction, because doors were opened to me that I had no idea even existed!

To begin carrying out my five-year plan, I interviewed 500 people in each of the four generations in the workplace while I traveled around the country for business. What an eye opener that was! I discovered that I hadn't stayed in touch with what twenty-somethings were interested in, and wanted in life and in the workplace. I discovered that this age group thought my age group was a bunch of old fogies who weren't willing to listen or learn. Wow; that was hard to take. But, I listened, and decided to capture the highlights of my research into a book so that other Baby Boomers and people older than I would have a clue about working effectively with younger generations. I had already successful published a book in 2002, a textbook that I wrote as a sole author. For this book, however, it occurred to me that my perspective alone wouldn't be sufficient because I wanted to build a bridge across several generations. So I thought about who might be a good co-author, and I didn't have to think too hard about my selection. Robin, a Generation Xer and former student of mine in a local university graduate program, was my choice. We began a year of writing and delivering presentations to all age groups that was invigorating, fun and fulfilling. Our book came out in January 2007, and Robin and I are still doing workshops and consulting on this important topic. A follow-up book is in process!

The opportunity for the book on emotional intelligence arrived from an unexpected source. I was delivering a workshop at the Toledo Zoo in 2004 for a colleague, Sheri, whom I'd met through my professional association. After the presentation, Sheri and I had lunch before I drove back to Cincinnati. During lunch, she shared that she'd always wanted to write a book, so I encouraged her to follow that dream. Then she floored me by saying, "Why don't we write a book together?" I thought very highly of Sheri, her keen mind, and great sense of humor. And, I was hooked on writing. So I said yes! We kicked around topics that interested us both, and right there at lunch we decided that emotional intelligence was an emerging field in relationship to its importance in the workplace. Even though at that time our experience in the field was limited, we decided to research the topic and write a book. We finished in late 2007, found a publisher in early 2008, and our book was released in early 2009. Sheri and I enjoyed working together tremendously, and we recently began research for writing another book together.

While Sheri and I were writing, another client and friend, John, shared the topic and content of his recent dissertation with me. I was intrigued by the leadership model he developed based on interviews of CEOs around the country, and I encouraged him to follow up with a book. You guessed it. He said, "So, why don't we write a book together?" Sheri and I finished writing our first manuscript draft on June 30, 2006. John and I began our collaboration on July 1, 2006. Did I have the good sense to give myself a break in between books? The answer is no, but addictions must be fed constantly. I couldn't help myself. John and I are finishing our book on leadership after an exciting two years of interviewing Fortune 500 CEOs, and it's in the hands of a publisher now, awaiting a release date.

By the way, Terri and I started writing our book the spring of 2007, while there was a lull in writing with my book with John. In case you're wondering, I get up at 5:00 a.m. every day of the week (yes, including Sunday), am ready to sit at my computer by 6:00 a.m., and I write or do research for a couple of hours. This disciplined approach has helped me do what I love for the past seven years—share my observations and experiences in written form. And yes, another colleague and I have plans to begin a book as soon as the manuscript for Just a Couple of Women Talkin' is finally in book form.

As a woman who just turned sixty, I've arrived at a place in my life that can best be summed up in one word: peace. I don't feel a need to assert myself all the time in order to get ahead. I don't feel a need to get my point of view across in every conversation. I don't feel a need to look perfect all the time (although I'm still pretty zealous about looking pulled together and professional). At a casual dinner party at my house a couple of years ago, a friend said to me, "You seem so calm, and when we first met a few years ago you were hyper . . . always on warp speed." I laughed and reminded her that I'm always moving fast because I live a busy life. It's just that I don't let people, events, and the usual bumps in the road get to me as much as when I was younger. When I'm in my "happy place," it's harder for me to allow other people to knock me into a place of anxiety or unnecessary angst. I think this attitude will work for you too, no matter what your age!

This calmer approach toward life has definitely affected my consulting in the last few years. I'm more likely to say what I think about a situation—in a more straightforward way than I did before. My clients are better off for this, because they're hiring me to be truthful from an objective, outside perspective. The companies that approach me with the notion that they want me to serve as a rubber stamp to their preconceived agenda don't get far with me. I politely say "no thanks" to the business.

7

What Am I Worth? How We Decided to Price Our Services

Many of the things you can count, don't count.
Many of the things you can't count, really count.
— Albert Einstein

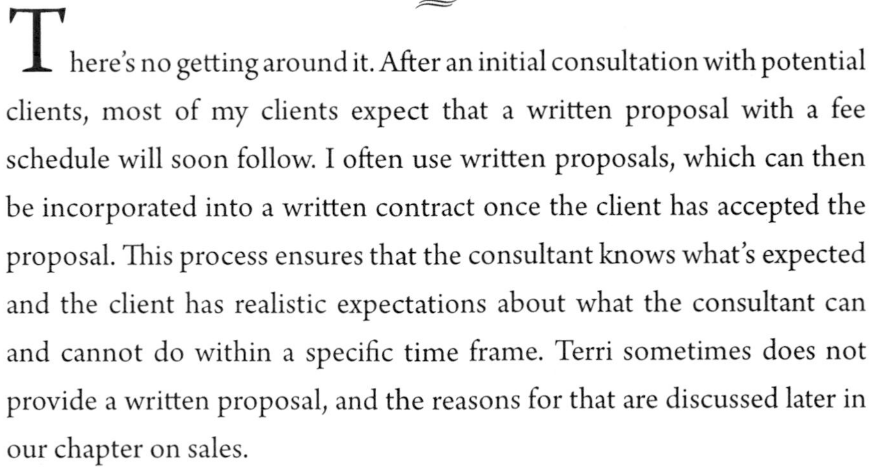

There's no getting around it. After an initial consultation with potential clients, most of my clients expect that a written proposal with a fee schedule will soon follow. I often use written proposals, which can then be incorporated into a written contract once the client has accepted the proposal. This process ensures that the consultant knows what's expected and the client has realistic expectations about what the consultant can and cannot do within a specific time frame. Terri sometimes does not provide a written proposal, and the reasons for that are discussed later in our chapter on sales.

When I receive a phone call or email from a potential client, I automatically pull out a client log sheet from my file cabinet (see Appendix 2). I learned to do this after the first three or four months of jotting down notes on Post-its when potential clients would call, only to discover when looking at the notes later that they weren't complete enough to prepare for our initial consultation. One time to visit a potential client's office without being fully prepared is one time too many.

The potential client log has not only the contact information, it has the project objectives, and a description of what the client wants (or thinks they want). The last item on the log contains action steps so that I or my team understand exactly what the next step in the process is — an initial consultation, a follow-up call in a month, etc.

The initial meeting with a potential client is critical for two reasons. First, it's the opportunity for you to "knock their socks off" with your background, expertise, and understanding of their needs. Secondly, it's the first chance you'll get to gather enough information to develop a written proposal that's comprehensive, clear, professional, and priced correctly.

Proposals can vary in length and content — it can be as short as one page or as long as twenty or more pages for government entities. (Entire books have been written on proposals and pricing for government contracts and because it's such a unique environment, we will not address it in this book.) A sample of one of my proposals is included in Appendix 3.

THE PRICING CHALLENGE

Based on our discussion with other consultants, we're not alone in concluding that pricing is one of the most challenging aspects of preparing a proposal. On the one hand, we want to be certain to make a living at what we're doing. On the other hand, we want to be realistic about the marketplace and what the organizations we want to work with can afford.

Recently, one of my consulting colleagues and I were having a casual phone conversation, catching up because we hadn't spoken with each other for quite some time. She was excited because she had just returned from a business trip, a speaking engagement for a company's in-house conference, located in a warm climate. My colleague is a good speaker; I've heard her speak on more than one occasion. She was pleased because she had asked for — and received — a $5,000 fee for doing a one-hour presentation. I was floored. Had I quoted a fee to do the same presentation (and I do have more than adequate experience speaking on the topic), I would have quoted a fee of $2,500. My first thought was, "I'm an idiot." My second thought was, "That's too much for this topic and for the time frame." Each of us has to research the marketplace and decide where we want to be within that framework: price leader, middle of the pack, or intentionally lower than average. I've elected to be a thought leader and high in terms of quality, yet I'm a middle-of-the-pack person in terms of pricing. There are just some organizations I want to work with that can't pay premium prices.

When pricing proposals, I have to balance the need to make a living and be paid a reasonable amount for my services and the need to "give back" to the community in the form of occasional lower-cost consulting. I believe it's important for all of us to feel valued, and to be paid what we're worth. I discovered that I had placed a boundary around this the first year I consulted.

Early on in my consulting career, I subcontracted with an established consulting firm for a few months. This seemed like a great way to learn from experienced consultants, since I was clueless about how to acquire clients and price proposals. The firm had existing clients that I could work with. I had a couple of clients I could bring into the organization and I would have access to a larger team with expertise to serve them in addition to mine. As I entered this arrangement, it seemed like a great way to go. It wasn't. My clients were paying a high hourly consulting rate for my work, yet I was receiving less that 50 percent of that rate by the time the consulting firm got its "cut." Additionally, I was paying a fee each month to have access to the firm's secretarial staff, whether I used them or not. After six months of working for one of my clients and actually not receiving one dime for the work, it occurred to me that this wasn't an equitable situation. Was it the consulting firm's fault? No. I didn't think things through carefully enough. I learned a hard but valuable lesson — I needed to be an astute business person and make sure I took care of my interests as well as my clients.

It's important to keep in mind that there are some organizations that have the resources to pay for the value they receive from consultants, and that's always such a pleasant surprise. In 2005, I was contacted by an organization that asked me to develop and facilitate a half-day training event for their managers. I'd learned by that point to inquire about a budget and the parameters the client had so that I didn't propose a fee that was simply out of reach (and I didn't want to "give way the store" either). My experience with similar organizations for a half-day workshop was that they would have a budget of about $1,500. The company representative came back with, "We really can't go over $3,000 — I hope we can convince you to do this for that amount." Mentally, I was thinking, "yippeeeeeeeeeeeeeeeeeeeeee," but I calmly said, "I'm willing to work within that framework." This company has been wonderful to work with over the past two years (actually, it doesn't feel like "work"), and it's great to have a balance of for-profit companies and nonprofits to even out the income stream.

If you'll look at the sample proposal, you'll see that the approach is to set out the project objectives (based on what the client shares in the initial consultation), estimate the time frame for completion, determine development time — for instance, to tailor workshops — and for delivery or client contact hours. You're not finished yet! Consider the value added to the client organization. If your consulting expertise will save the client thousands of dollars, that's worth money beyond the hours you're with the client. In other words, don't charge for four hours of contact time x $200/hour = $800 if your unique expertise and ideas for implementation will allow the client to save $100,000! Charge for the contact hours and a percentage of projected savings (a reasonable range is 10 – 25 percent).

You've probably been wondering as you're reading along here, "So how do I know what the market price is for my consulting services?" It's true that you probably can't call just any consultant by pulling a name from the phone book and saying, "Hi there . . . I'm one of your competitors and I'd like to know what you charge so I can be competitive with my pricing." There are other ways to discover what consultants in your area (or other areas of the country) are charging. For example, if you're a Human Resource Management consultant, the Society for Human Resource Management (SHRM) has a Consultant's Forum, which I joined several years ago. Membership provides consultants with articles written by experts in the field on a wide range of interesting topics, as well as discounts for purchases such as office equipment and information about health insurance and other benefits. Consultants can also be listed in SHRM's online directory so that SHRM members looking for services have easy access to contact information and a short bio. Here's their web site: http://www.shrm.org/consultants.

Terri and I save brochures for workshops and consultation services that hit our desk, at least long enough to compare what other consultants are doing with our services and to check out the fee schedule listed on the brochure. We keep a worksheet with prices so that, at least once a year, we can revisit our pricing schedule to see if we're where we want to be, and confirm that we're in the market range for services.

What about the cost of client entertainment, you might be wondering. This can range from dinners out at a country club to grabbing a hot dog at the airport. I've done both . . . and everything in between. Something I had to think about early on was how to budget for client entertainment and whether to include working lunches or dinner with clients in invoicing back to the client company or pick up the tab and expense the money on my tax return. Let me tell you a couple of stories, one from my first week as a consultant.

The current HR director for a company I had worked for a few years before called me and asked if she could meet me for lunch. She said that she had heard I'd started a consulting practice and was interested in talking with me about coming to the company as a workshop presenter for a management topic. I knew this lady slightly through a professional association but she was not someone I knew well. As I was walking from my car to the coffee shop where we agreed to meet, it struck me that I had no idea if I was expected to pick up the bill. It wasn't a "sit down" restaurant; you ordered sandwiches from a window. If I arrived first, should I wait for her so we could go up to the window together and I could pay for both lunches? I agonized for the entire five-minute walk because I wanted to do the courteous thing, but didn't want her to think I was "buying" her business! (Could you "buy" someone's business with a $2.50 sandwich?) As I walked into the restaurant, she was already there, and we walked up to the order window together as we chatted. I simply said, "I'll treat," and it was as easy as that. Since that time, I don't agonize over the situation; however, I do think about how to handle situations like that in advance.

When in doubt, I opt for picking up the tab (and expensing it or making it a tax write off).

Sometimes, my clients have an expense account for working lunches or dinners. When their team, including me as their consultant, goes out to lunch or dinner and we continue to work during that time, the client pulls out a company credit card and pays for the entire group. The first time this situation occurred, I had been consulting for about three months. A group of six managers and I were planning a retreat that I would be facilitating. The meeting ran into the lunch hour, so the person who invited me to work with the company announced that we were all going to lunch to continue our work while we ate. I was thinking, "Oh man, does my credit card have enough on it to pay for lunch for seven?!" I had exactly enough cash with me to get my car out of the garage, and I was pretty sure ten dollars wouldn't go far at the restaurant the group decided on. Bless his heart, as we sat down at the table, the company rep told me that he would put the bill on his company's card. I wondered if the relief I felt was too obvious.

BASIC PRICING

Terri

Fresh from college with a 4.0 in my business classes, and with all the new ideas my head could hold, I was eager to apply my new learning. I immediately went to see my Dad about how I could improve his business. At age twenty-five, I wanted to revamp his entire business; I was especially excited about marketing and pricing.

I soon learned that in my hometown (population 2,600) marketing consisted of reputation, reputation, reputation. Everyone knew or was related to everyone else. No marketing necessary. (Dad twice ran for city council and won handily without any campaigning, not a single yard sign, and no campaign fund.)

Pricing and profitability were related to that reputation. While I was growing up, Dad was the only plumber in town. His closest competitor was thirty miles away. He wasn't a casual laborer — he had gone to college before he started his business and night school while he was working to become a certified Master Plumber. Even as competition emerged in that town, other plumbers didn't match his credentials or his service. By the time I completed college, my dad had twenty-five years of experience in residential plumbing, several commercial jobs under his belt and he had added heating and air conditioning to his service offerings. During the time that I remember, he always charged the same amount for his labor.

I tried to convince Dad that he could charge more — his most significant competitors were charging twenty dollars an hour more. He would have no part of it. His reasons were either his neighbors couldn't afford more or he didn't need more.

When my dad retired at age seventy-two, I think he was still charging the same hourly rate.

As a result of my dad's attitude, I learned that the magic range of pricing a service lies somewhere between what the market will bear and what you need.

≈

PRICING AS A PROCESS

Pricing is a process, like most business activities. The following process is one that you can follow at the beginning of your practice, and later as you evaluate the changes in your life and your business. Here is a process that I have found helpful:

1. Discovery and Intentions;
2. Organization and Time Practices;
3. Quantitative and Qualitative Research;
4. Differentiation and Branding; and
5. Running the Numbers.

DISCOVERY AND INTENTIONS

"We are told that talent creates its own opportunities. But it sometimes seems that intense desire creates not only its own opportunities, but its own talents."

—Eric Hoffer

Ideally, you begin by discovering what you really want and identifying how much you want it. Writing your own professional script allows you to identify and validate what is important to you, as well as how intensely you will pursue it. Like a great novel, your story script has a beginning, a middle, and an end. How will you get started? What will be your crowning achievement? When the time comes, how will you let go of your business?

DISCOVERY

Discovery means learning as much about yourself as possible. Spend some reflection time and document what you know about yourself. What are your strengths, the skills that you possess, and the things that you are less than stellar at performing? This exercise will provide you with some ideas about which items of your business you will perform yourself, and what you will outsource. Outline for yourself what is important to you in this new endeavor and in your life. This is a whole-life exercise.

These are the questions that I have found helpful in the discovery process:

- → What are your financial needs?
- → How much money do you want to put in your own pocket from your business?
- → What are your non-financial needs?
- → Travel? Business and personal?

→ More family time?

→ Community service?

→ Vacation or other time off?

Let's take an example:

You want to make $100,000 annually for yourself, after all business expenses and taxes.

You want travel out of your community limited to 10 percent of the time.

You want to spend two more hours per day with your family, without intruding on your current six hours of sleep per night.

You want to serve on one civic board of directors.

You want to take off four weeks each year.

You will notice that all of your needs are number specific. These numbers are important to completing the *Time and Intention Matrix* on the following pages.

INTENTIONS

Next, what are your intentions? Your intentions are the declarations to yourself (and eventually to others) about what you want to do. Intentions are your compass. They provide direction, and are best developed in advance of your activities to pursue your goals. Your values are a part of this process. Values are the boundaries for moving toward your intentions. An example of values is operating with honesty and integrity. (Reminding yourself of your values also reduces the risk of violating your boundaries, as several public figures have reportedly done this year. I call the violation of the public/private trust ethical drift.)

Completing this sentence may help: I intend to ______________ ______________ and ______________________________ by ______________ ______________ and ______________________, following the boundaries

of my values: ________________, ________________, __________
______, and ______________________.

Some people refer to this as a personal mission statement.

PLANS AND PRACTICES

You can list all of your needs and your intentions, place them in priority, and assign a value to them, such as 1) must-have, 2) like-to-have, and 3) nice-to-have.

For example, you must have $50,000 a year, like to have $75,000 and it would be nice to have $100,000. You want two more hours a day to spend with your children, but the first hour after school you consider as a must-have. You want to serve on a civic board of directors, and most organizations require that you also serve on a committee as well. That will take from two to eight hours per month. You must have four weeks of vacation this year, so that you can travel with your husband to Europe for your tenth wedding anniversary trip. You love to travel, but traveling for business will take you away from spending time with your children, so limited business travel is all that you want to do. So, the business travel must-have is limited to 10 percent, like-to-have is 5 percent, and nice-to-have zero percent.

As you can tell, these priorities can change from year-to-year — you're not going to take another anniversary trip to Europe to celebrate the eleventh year of your marriage — even if it would be nice to do so. Once your children are grown, business travel may once again become attractive.

Once you have spent some reflection time in identifying your personal strengths and what is truly important to you, you will declare your intentions. Next in the process are your organization and time practices.

Once you identify these, you can develop a matrix that will demonstrate how these two concepts work together.

ORGANIZATION AND TIME PRACTICES

Available time is a critical factor in your pricing. For example, if a consultant has chosen to work in her own business so that she can spend more time with her family, then she may have to reduce the amount of time that can be deployed on behalf of her business. However, this could work in reverse. If you were working seventy hours a week in your previous job, with a 20 percent reduction in hours, you would still have fifty-six hours per week available to work — far more than the standard of forty.

Each individual is different in her or his desire for both time and money. A survey reported in 2000 that the largest percentage of respondents (28.3 percent) indicated they were willing to make up to 20 percent less money in order to create more balance in their lives.[43] However, a survey of younger women (ages 22 to 35) in 2010, showed women seeking more time, have somewhat higher incomes, and willing to forego 15 percent of their income, while respondents willing to sacrifice time want a 32 percent increase in salary.

Therefore, what the trade-off in time and money from 15-20 percent means is unique to each individual and presumably, age and stage of life.

I was working seventy to eighty hours a week when I was in corporate America, a reduction from 100 hours per week during a merger. I wanted to work fewer hours, and fewer specific hours. When I began Just The Basics®, I realized I could shift time, most days, so that I could stop work at 3:30 p.m. each afternoon to spend more time with my son after he got home from school. However, I also found myself taking an entire week (or weeks at a time) to attend to ailing and elderly family members. I also found that many people make or return afternoon calls only after checking-in with their children once they arrive home from school. Therefore, I made or returned those calls, either at 4:30 p.m. when my son went out to play or the first thing the following morning.

It bears mentioning again that family members and friends sometimes assume that working for yourself means that you can take on other family responsibilities. If we see ourselves as primary caregivers, we have to be careful about setting our own boundaries. If we are primary income earners, we also have to be careful about those boundaries. If we are both primary caregivers and primary income earners, we have even less time to devote to anything except those activities and to our own personal needs. By boundaries, we mean respecting and honoring our own needs.

If we do not respect and honor our own needs, neither will others. We risk major health issues if we overload ourselves with both care-giving and high earnings expectations.[44] Most people are familiar the instructions that airline attendants give us as we take off in the airplane: "Be sure to place the (oxygen) mask on yourself first, then your child." If you don't take good care of yourself, others will not be able to depend on you.

The following matrix may be helpful in calculating, thus far, your organization and time practices along with your discovery and intentions:

TIME AND INTENTION MATRIX

	Must Have	Like To Have	Nice To Have	Probably Will Have
Income	$200,000	$300,000	$400,000	$250,000
Profit (25%)	$50,000	$75,000	$100,000	$62,500
Work Travel	Whatever is required	5%	0%	30%
Time At Home	4 hours per day	6 hours per day	8 hours per day	6 hours per day when not traveling
Personal Travel	0	Three weeks	Four weeks	Two weeks
Work Hours	Whatever is required	50 hours per week	40 hours per week	70 hours per week

The third step in the Pricing Process is research.

RESEARCH: QUALITATIVE AND QUANTITATIVE

"Before we build a better mousetrap, we need to find out if there are any mice out there."
—Yogi Berra

Before establishing your price, you may want to conduct research about the market rate for the services you provide. Some research is free, some inexpensive and some expensive. However, mistakes in determining the type of research can be the most expensive.

Before you determine the type of market research necessary for your pricing strategy, you need to identify as specifically as you can certain categories, including your level of expertise, as well as the range and the specific products and services that you offer. Let's take a look at an example before we proceed to the types of research that are available.

We have used human resources as an example in most situations because that is a joint skill and what we both know well. The major categories will be the same for any consulting field, but the detail provided below is specific to our field.

An example in the field of Human Resources:

1. Category: Level of expertise:
    a. Compensation specialist;
    b. Generalist; or
    c. Recruiter.
2. Category: Range of products and services provided:
    a. By-product line; and/or
    b. By-service line.
3. Category: Specific products and services:

a. Executive compensation, sales compensation, wage and salary administration plans;
b. Sales recruiter;
c. Food and beverage industry recruiter; or
d. Administrative assistant and secretarial recruiter.

More specific examples of these services and expanded areas of expertise are included in Appendix 4. Additionally, the "Human Resource Skills Assessment" in Appendix 5 [45] may be helpful to HR professionals as a tool to determine both your level of expertise and the areas in which you wish to consult. These are not necessarily the same. For example, my skills in HR administration are outstanding; however, I do not like to do it, nor is it an effective use of my time. Therefore, while I have the expertise, I am not willing to provide consulting in the administrative functions of human resources; so, I don't.

OTHER QUESTIONS

Here are a few more questions before you determine your method of pricing strategy research:

- Who do you want to purchase your products and services?
- Who is purchasing them now?
- Can your target purchaser authorize the purchase of your products and services?

For example, are you targeting the CEO, the president, the HR director, or the training director? If you were a compensation specialist in a large organization, your experience may not get you access to the president of a large corporation (but the HR director may be able to authorize the purchase of your services). If you were a corporate vice president, and now run your own company, your level of expertise and your current title may get you into the CEO's office. If you were a training specialist and are a training consultant, you can reasonably expect to be able to get into a training director's office. The decision maker you can reach with the products and services that you offer will determine who you should target in your market research efforts. For example, in our market two women decided to open their own consulting firms: one had been an excellent compensation director for a Fortune 500 firm; the other a trainer for a separate medium sized firm. Their titles were both "managing director." Their target was the CEO of large firms. However, even with excellent credentials, they could not reach the CEOs of those firms. You can imagine what may have made a difference — a title of President and Vice President may have helped. Targeting the HR director first may have helped to eventually reach the CEO's office. Or, making their offerings more narrow, say on compensation and training, rather than a broader range of expansive HR services. Eventually, their combined practice became a consortium of consultants and services, but the firm never reached the potential they dreamed of – that of a full-service, strategic HR firm with large company clients.

Now, let's review the types of research and their price ranges.

TYPES OF MARKET RESEARCH

"Doing your research didn't end when formal schooling ended. Homework is a part of life-long learning."

—Terri Bonar-Stewart

Market research falls into two categories: qualitative (quality) and quantitative (the numbers). Research is essential to accurately determine market pricing, specifically, market pricing research for services similar to the ones you provide.

As we said earlier, market research does not have to be expensive to be effective. Secondary sources, such as published surveys, articles or white papers, or informed experts[vi] can be used. Your prospects and clients may tap those same sources to determine what they are willing to pay and what the market rate is for the services they are seeking. Additional market research may also be available at no cost from the Small Business Administration (SBA), or the Service Corps of Retired Executives (SCORE). Or, as Linda mentioned earlier, targeted information sources such as a trade association (SHRM in our case) or generalized domain sources for consulting services offer relevant guidelines.

More traditional market research techniques include focus groups, phone surveys, and in-person interviews. One type is the "Voice of the Customer" survey. The process includes:

- Establishing objectives;
- Development and revision of the questions; and
- Conducting the interviews.

Key patterns will emerge to determine what your customers find of value. Sometimes what customers find of value is not the same as what the consultant believes that she is offering.

During my strategic planning effort after five years in the business, I used a more simple technique: I asked clients and colleagues to describe my firm's most valuable services in three words. I was surprised to learn that the most common attributes were not limited to my technical skills, but the following:

→ Guidance,
→ Clarity,

vi Informed experts are individuals in the marketplace, such as bankers, attorney, accountants, and friends in the market who purchase consulting services or have clients who purchase consulting services.

- → Insight,
- → Encouragement,
- → Intelligence,
- → Tools,
- → Techniques,
- → Truth,
- → Confidentiality, and
- → Results

Based on this data, I began to change the focus of Just The Basics® to build my business (including my pricing and marketing strategy) on the concepts that were most valued by my clients.

MARKET RESEARCH: QUALITATIVE AND QUANTITATIVE DATA

More commonly in market research, when time and budget allow, a three-step process is used — interviews, focus groups, and more targeted written surveys. The interviews and focus groups provide qualitative information; the written survey, quantitative data.

The market research strategy employed and the tactics chosen will be based on: time and budget constraints, goals, learning objectives, and what you will do with the data.

Once you have completed your discovery and identified your intentions, your time and intention matrix, and your market research, you can proceed to the creating your unique business proposition — your branding. Branding is important to commanding the highest prices for your products and services.

DIFFERENTIATION AND BRANDING

"Do not go where the path may lead, go instead where there is no path and leave a trail."
—Ralph Waldo Emerson

Even a small difference in an area of concentration can make a big difference in pricing your business services. Even though Terri provides many of the same services as other consultants to management, Terri's target markets are small businesses, nonprofits and associations. These organizations seldom have a HR professional on staff, so her differentiation factors are her approach and entrée to the organization with HR consulting. She avoids traditional HR terms, unless necessary; and translates the typical HR terms that the CEO may hear in the marketplace; and designs simplified versions of HR activities and tasks, frequently recommending no-cost, low-cost human resource alternatives. Then, Terri builds and nurtures relationships with the presidents and executive directors, and eventually is asked to work on a higher, more strategic level with them and their boards of directors

What is different about the product or service that you offer and that of your competition? Differentiation may offer you the opportunity to charge a different rate than your competition. This will only be true if you understand what is different and unique about your services, and whether you can effectively market that differentiating factor. The following are potential differentiating factors:

- Product and service mix;
- Level of decision-maker you can access;
- Type of business — for profit, nonprofit, small, medium and large organizations;

- Type of industry you serve; and
- Sector within that industry.

Differentiation can lead consultants to brand their product or service. Terri's company name is trademarked, for example. Her written articles (and this book) are copyrighted.

Linda's company name is not copyrighted because it's her own name (Gravett and Associates). She made her husband promise not to object to her using the name, even if he loses his mind, leaves her and takes another wife with the last name of Linda's business.

Differentiation leads to branding, whether formal or informal. A brand can make it easier to sell your services and products, easier to set higher prices, and it's often a way of protecting your assets. Not only is protecting your assets advisable, it can be financially rewarding should you decide to sell or merge your firm. Recognized branded products or services can be valued separately and much more easily than "good will" in such a transaction. (Remember that we are planning for the end of the story as well as the beginning.)

RUNNING THE NUMBERS AND PROJECT PRICING

Having taken the time to determine your unique offerings and branding your company and services, you are now ready to run the numbers for your basic business plan, financial plans, and individual project pricing. Basic pricing involves the discipline to sit down with a spreadsheet, document some assumptions, and run some numbers. The local Small Business Development Center or your accountant can help.

REFINING YOUR NUMBERS

There are options to hourly billing pricing and the use of alternative pricing is a growing phenomenon. The numbers can be refined as different types of pricing: hourly, project cost fixed fee, cost plus fixed fee, or variable pricing. We have learned that the following forms of pricing are the most common:

Hourly rate — a fee charged by the hour of work, as outlined below;

Project cost fixed fee — a fixed fee for a project based on understanding the scope of the work and the products desired (commonly called the deliverables);

Cost plus fixed fee — direct costs plus a percentage or a fixed amount of dollars over and above your costs;

Variable pricing — based on several flexible options once a true understanding of costs, the cost-savings and potential revenue streams are realized, pricing to the individual client and project; and

Fixed fee plus a percentage of savings — a pricing option after implementation. (Note: the consultant takes a big risk in pricing in this manner since the implementation is normally up to the CEO and there is no guarantee that the CEO will actually implement the recommendations.)

There is also "trusted advisor" status that takes a consultant beyond the realm of specific technical consulting and into the role of guiding the client, the business, and occasionally the operating environment: Here, the consultant is going beyond the specialty into business consulting, sometimes referred to as management consulting. In our practices, we have advised clients on the naming of their business, work processes, and facility and workspace design (working with the architect to maximize communication between employees). Additionally, we have advised clients to use a payroll service, to hire a bookkeeper instead of CPA, or to hire a CPA instead of a bookkeeper. We have made recommendations regarding marketing, sales, commercial realtors, etc. These are not the average HR consultant practice areas, but our clients requested these services and trusted us to advise them on these issues. Trusted advisor status requires an extensive and well-developed network of colleagues in several fields.

Trusted advisor status can result in adjustment of fees, both up and down. The concept is to have the client think of you first every time she doesn't have a resource to solve the problem – whatever it is. Your network is key to helping the client where you personally do not have the expertise. This keeps you top-of-mind, which is where all consultants would like to be.

Another choice in pricing strategy is outlined in Alan Weiss's book *Value-Based Fees.*[46] Alan expresses it so well that trying to summarize his book in three sentences is beyond good sense. However, to provide you with a sense of his book, we quote from the book jacket, "perceived value is the basis of the fee . . . (the consultant) must translate the importance of their advice into long-term gains for the client in the client's perception. *Value-Based Fees* shows consultants how to easily and adroitly educate clients about value determining worth and consequent investment." We encourage you to read his book for a complete understanding.

Once you have determined your pricing philosophy, your needs, your intentions, then conducted your research and run your numbers, you have the basis for your individual project pricing. You know what you want, need and can afford to do. The following section outlines some common project pricing.

HOURLY RATE BILLING

For hourly rate billing (and for more information in estimating pricing variations), the following are some considerations:

Time Assets:

Total Available Hours

Billable Hours

Non-Billable Hours:

  Applied Time Hours

  Non-Applied Time Hours, i.e., vacation, training, research

  Miscellaneous, i.e., administrative tasks

Billable Rates:

  Book Rate

Published Rate

Discounts: i.e., Established Customers, Long-term Projects, Non-Profit Organizations

New Client Rate

Realization Rate (actual average billed rate)

Personal Assets:

Expert Status

Education, Training and Credentialing

Consider the additional detail we've presented below:

TIME ASSETS: TOTAL AVAILABLE HOURS

A baseline for the average available hours is normally 2,080 hours per year. This is calculated by taking the average work week of 40 hours times 52 weeks per year. This is the basis of most "available to work" targets.

However, reduced by an average two week vacation (40 hours a week for two weeks) equals 2,000 hours per year. Additionally, the available work time can be reduced by holidays, especially when calculating available time for employees.

Our experience suggests that business owners tend to work many holidays. Owners frequently find that without employees on the premises, holidays are a good time to do a few things they normally do not fit into their schedules — that means exploring some ideas about additional employee development or revising that employee handbook.

As an owner, you can determine how many holidays you intend to observe, remembering that maintaining a happy home and family are also likely "success goals." You may also want to refer back to your Time and Intention Matrix in this section before determining your available time.

TRADITIONAL CONSULTING PRICING

A detailed example of hourly billing rates, multiple rates and profitability is below:

MULTIPLE RATES AND PROFITABILITY

Most consulting firms have multiple rates. There is the documented or quoted rate, sometimes referred to as the list rate. This is also referred to as the (hourly) book rate and is the full, billable rate with no discounts applied. Many times the book rate is for small projects or short-term projects. Rates may be reduced when a longer-term project or large project is contracted. Rate reductions are referred to as a discounted rate. There may be book rate for new clients, while former clients stay at different rate, resulting in a discount rate for current clients. Additionally, there may be a reduced rate for non-profit organizations.

Therefore, a consultant may have a high billable rate but still be generating poor profits. This occurs when a consultant has been billed out at a low hourly rate, due to discounts or applied, but not billable hours.

Hours may be "applied" but not billed. After billable work, most consultants apply their time to unbillable customer work. Consultants are expected to maintain customer satisfaction. Keeping up with client industry trends or taking clients to lunch may not be billable, but seldom is this time wasted when customer satisfaction is the goal. Alternately, doing research for a client that may not billable may be appropriate if the research is to provide an improved product and/or can be used later with several clients.

It is important, however, to understand how much time is being invested in customer accounts. There is a real economic impact on the organization to support this investment. By tracking these hours, the firm can determine if this investment is providing the value intended.

The applied, but not billable, hours should be limited to initiatives and activities that have value to the company.

Well-priced consulting practices that use this method have "adjusted" time goals, which include:

- Available hours
- Billable hours
- Applied time hours
- Training and development hours
- Miscellaneous
- Targeted adjusted achievement rate hours

The adjusted time goals that result in the adjusted achievement rate, when met, are a key factor in hourly rate billing profitability.

An example of the adjusted achievement rate follows:

- Available annual work hours: 100 percent
- Billable Hour Goal: 60 percent
- Applied Time Goal: 10 percent
- Business Development Goal: 25 percent
- Training and Development Hours: 2.5 percent
- Miscellaneous: 2.5 percent

By following this exercise, you have probably concluded that there are fewer hours available for billing than you first imagined. The only way to increase your billable hours is to work more hours. At 2000 (2080 work hours per year minus 80 hours for vacation) you can see that perhaps 60 percent of your hours are billable. According to multiple sources, 60 percent is a solid billable goal for experienced consultants.

The following chart depicts Available Time. Once available time is determined, next is the calculation of billable hours.

Categories/ Ranking: 5 highest; 1 lowest	Mine	Market Average	Market Maximum	$ Likely
Education, Training, Credentials				
Expert Status				
Time Availability				

TIME ASSETS: BILLABLE HOURS AND NON-BILLABLE HOURS

It is relatively easy to calculate billable hours. The challenge is determining the number of hours for which the client can be billed versus the time that cannot be billed. For example, sometimes a consultant performs work related to a client's project (such as research), but cannot bill the customer for that time, so it should not be included in the calculation of the billable hours.

Sometimes, a client will pay for your research and development time. In 2008, Terri had a referred prospect that asked if she had experience in the development of a traditional HR product, but in a new delivery format. She told him that she had thirty years' experience in the product area, but none in the specific delivery system (a new technology) he wanted. She continued to explain that if he would describe his project to her, perhaps she could refer him to someone who could help. By the time the phone conversation was finished, he had asked to meet her in person, and said he would cover the cost of her research and development for this project since her experience in the subject matter was already so deep.

Before meeting the client the following week, she did significant research, enlisting the help of a technology expert, and prepared herself to ask the client "intelligent" questions based on her research. She did not charge him for this research time; but, she planned and advised the client that she intended to charge him for the time that it took to translate her "deep subject matter" experience into the delivery system format. That seemed fair to both of them.

Remember that your billable hours may not be at your book (or published) rate. Here is an example:

Book Rate	Non Profit Book Rate	New Client Book Rate	Preferred Client Rate	Average Billable Rate (last year)
$100	$80	$120	$90	$85
			Discount for long-established clients	
Also called the quoted, list or documented rate	A discount, normally a percentage decrease over the book rate.	A higher rate for new clients than for existing clients	Discount also applied for longer-term or larger projects.	The average of actual billed rates last year.

PERSONAL ASSETS

Expert Status

Expert status involves two elements. The first is the type and level of experience in a particular area that a consultant brings to the table. The second element is perspective — a point of view from the outside looking in. Perspective comes from the conscious consideration of the consultant's personal life experience, knowledge derived from other client projects, and from research and reading.

Expert status may also include special skills and abilities that others may not possess.

Education, Training and Credentialing — The amount of education and training that you have, as well as the credentials you possess, are the basis for a pricing differential. Certifications and education may garner more income in some cases; in others, specific expertise may have the edge in pricing.

Time Availability Revisited — Time availability was covered earlier in this chapter; refer to the prior section to determine and chart your own personal asset analysis.

Initially, for example, Terri found that her expert status ranked at the market maximum, her education, training and credentials in the middle range, and time availability in the lower range. Therefore, she reasoned, her pricing should reflect each of these and she priced her services at the low-average range of the market. Once her time availability increased and therefore, her flexibility increased, Terri raised her prices to the market average range.

We have determined that being the low-cost provider of services is not much different than the low cost provider of products. In both cases, the market's perception of your value is undermined, and in the consulting business, volume does not make up for lost profits. There are few cost reductions available in a service business. Resource reductions are difficult when the primary asset is you.

These are consulting-specific pricing alternatives. They don't include the frequently coupled speaking, facilitating or training assignments.

PRICING SPEAKING, TRAINING, AND FACILITATION NOTES

Some quick notes regarding speaking, training and facilitation pricing. Most importantly, it is easy to underestimate the time involved for each of these activities. While we will not give this topic a complete treatment, here are some quick tips:

1. Traditional training price guidelines include four hours preparation for each hour of training, and similar numbers for speaking engagements. Additionally, there is planning time involved prior to the training in collaboration with the client, and a debriefing time following the training.
2. Facilitation also requires pre-work and it can be estimated at two to three hours preparation for each hour of facilitation. Debriefing time is common following a facilitation engagement.
3. Prior to any speech, it is imperative that you understand the underlying goal of the event, as well as the who, what, where, when, why, and how of the event being planned.

Whether training, speaking or facilitating, planning is necessary to prevent client disappointment as well as under billing your efforts.

ONE IMPORTANT ADDITIONAL PRICING OPTION

Pricing is one of the most arduous tasks facing consultants. Here's yet another method—an additional layer of considerations beyond the traditional options—we've used to determine pricing strategy:

Questions to ask yourself before quoting a price to a customer:

1. Who referred me?
2. What is the nature of the relationship with the referral source?
3. What is the time line of the decision?

4. What are the impending deadlines driving the decision to engage a consultant?
5. Who is paying for the service?
6. Where do they fall on the organization chart?
    a. Formally?
    b. Informally?
7. How profitable is the organization?
8. How long has the organization been in business?
9. How sophisticated is the client in relation to my services?
10. Does this client add to my firm's skills, or am I using existing skills?
11. Does this client open up a new niche or market segment for the firm?
12. Do I like this client?
13. Should I include a pain tolerance factor?
14. Is this client in a business that I am interested in?
15. Are the goals, objectives, outputs (desired products) and outcomes (desired results) clear and unambiguous?
16. Is there a rush on this project?
17. Should I include a pricing rush-factor?
18. What price do I <u>want</u> to charge the customer?

RECAP

While we have provided a great deal of information on pricing your consulting services, our goal is to use the Alan Weiss pricing model of value-based fees. As HR consulting becomes more valued, and placing a value on the services we provide becomes more common, we predict this pricing model will become more popular with both clients and consultants. Anecdotal information suggests that on both the East and West Coasts, this pricing model has made significant inroads into consulting practices. In our local market, we have the ongoing challenge of client education on this topic. Nevertheless, it is important to understand the pricing terminology and your motivation in pricing before choosing any particular method(s) for your business.

THE MOST SUCCESSFUL CONSULTING ASSIGNMENTS

The most successful consulting engagements are those to which both parties agree to the problem, the intent, the process, the products (the outputs) and the outcomes (the results), and the measures of success. The consultant and the client act as equal partners, and both become the owner of the problem and the solution. An on-going dialogue is required to reach the best products and results.

At the end of any project, both parties should understand and discuss the results. Some of the more common results that can be evaluated are:

1. Client knowledge and skill acquisition,
2. Business unit or organizational impact, and
3. Return on Investment.

Ideally, client satisfaction and intangible benefits are also evaluated.

The final agreement on the results, how they are to be measured, and how well the expectations were met, form the basis of the worth of the project. Pricing based on these concepts provides the most value to both the client and the consultants. Consultants deserve to reap the rewards of work well done, of products delivered, and results accomplishments.

8

Always Be Selling: Our Philosophy on Sales

"Always be selling."

—Quote from the 1992 movie, *Glengarry Glen Ross*.

Many women we've talked with over the years have decided against consulting for one reason: aversion to sales. Make no mistake, consultants must be involved in sales both directly and indirectly in order to grow the business. In this chapter, we'll provide some ideas about what has worked for us and our colleagues.

inda

My stomach was tied up in knots. I was more nervous than I'd been —for any reason —in years. Why? I was about to make my first sales call as a consultant. It was my first day of my first week, and I'd been referred to my potential client by a consultant friend. My friend didn't work in the area the client wanted, so she referred the company to me. I had set up the initial meeting to meet the client, explore their needs, and share my ability to serve these needs. Today this type of meeting doesn't faze me in the least because I'm confident about what I can and cannot provide for clients—and that confidence has come from experience in actually completing projects and measuring the success against established objectives. That day, I literally had to stand outside the client's door and take a few deep breaths to collect myself before I entered. (P.S. I didn't get the project because my expertise wasn't a good fit; however, I learned a lot about sales calls and I'll be sharing those tidbits in this chapter.)

There are several ways to go about selling in the consulting arena. Some consultants make "cold calls," either in person or by letter, to companies they believe might have a need for their services. Two schools of thought prevail on this: one, send out many, many letters or knock on hundreds of doors and you'll eventually get lucky; and two, do lots of research on potential companies and target a few likely candidates to call or write. Most of our female colleagues do not spend much time on "cold calls," and there's one primary reason for this—they hate rejection.

On the one hand, making "cold" phone calls or writing letters to people you don't know shows initiative. You have the opportunity to collect your thoughts and pull together marketing materials in a thoughtful way when you're mailing a letter, brochures and testimonials. On the other hand, letters must be precise and impeccable, with highly tailored and targeted information that will grab the reader's attention (assuming someone actually reads your letter). If you elect to contact potential clients using this approach, it's necessary to follow up one, two, three, or even more times. It's hard to know what the boundary is between being acceptably assertive and coming across as pushy and annoying.

If you are fortunate enough to get a sales appointment with a decision maker, either through a referral or letter campaign, we'd like to share some thoughts about making an excellent impression.

Consider offering a one hour complimentary consultation in order to get to know the company representative and gather information about their needs. This gives you an opportunity to observe the company culture and have "face time" with at least one person that you might be working with. Use the time to collect data that can be used to prepare a proposal, which you would send to the company within a mutually agreed time after the meeting. Our caution here is that you don't "give away the store" during this meeting by providing an entire afternoon's worth of free consulting. It's easy for potential clients to start talking about their problems and for you to launch into consulting mode with solutions, right then and there. Fight that urge. Share your approach and philosophy toward dealing with issues, but wait to start consulting until you have a contract!

Once you're in the lobby of your potential client's organization, normally a receptionist or an administrative support person will greet you. Be nice to them; these folks are the gatekeepers to important people within the company. We know executives who lean heavily on their administrative support staff to let them know about potential consultants' manners and professional demeanor during their time waiting for their appointment. Make a good impression, starting in the first seven seconds you walk in the door, by courteously greeting the staff you meet and being friendly and polite.

Speaking of good impressions, I've done research over the last several years about the perception people draw of others they meet for the first time. Through my research, I discovered a "7/11 Rule" which works like this: people form at least eleven impressions of you within the first seven seconds they meet you. That's not long to form a positive impression, which means your dress, your grooming, and your demeanor need to be appropriate to the setting.

During initial sales calls, put on your listening ears. When you talk, it should be to ask questions and clarify points. When the potential client asks you about your experience and expertise, that's the time to provide information on experiences you've had that are similar to what the client is dealing with. The client doesn't want a long history of your "pedigree," rather the client wants to know what you can do to address their problems or meet their needs. Watch for body language cues so that you know when to stop talking; that is when the sale is made.

I was in an initial sales call with an associate, and we had asked for and received time on the potential client's schedule for thirty minutes to make our "pitch." We agreed ahead of time which role each person would take, and I was first. My associate was the "closer" with a brief presentation about how our organization could provide them with guidance and an approach that would be tailored and cost-effective. My associate did just fine with that piece, and our allotted time was almost over. The potential client thanked us for our presentation, and let us know that she was indeed impressed and would take our "leave-behind" and notes from our meeting to her executive team. That was our cue to say our thank you and exit gracefully. But, my colleague took a breath and dove back in, with a discussion about a similar initiative our company had undertaken that the client may also find of interest. My "read" of the client's body language told me that she was already mentally off to her next appointment, so I jumped in when my associate took a breath and said, "We'll be sure to share more information about this part of our business when we have more time," and I started to stand up. My colleague kept on talking, so I had to actually talk over him! I made a joke by saying, "As you can see, my associate is really excited about working with you." Finally, he got the hint, and also said his thank you and goodbye.

The concept of pacing has long been a technique used by sales people everywhere. Here's how it works: If the person you're meeting tends to be energetic and talk rapidly, you pick up your energy level to match theirs. If the person you're meeting focuses on core values and beliefs, you share how your core values and beliefs align with theirs (if they do). There's a misconception that sales people should build rapport by, for instance, noticing a child's picture and commenting about their own children of similar age. You can waste ten minutes of a one-hour meeting this way. I'd rather relate to clients by researching a challenge or issue they face and opening with a discussion around that topic. Of course, this approach takes some research and definitely calls for you to interact on a case-by-case basis; one size doesn't fit all here.

Provide a "leave behind" for the potential client that represents you positively. This could be a brochure, an article that addresses the topic of your meeting, or a web site you would recommend as a resource. You might consider a packet that has separate sections that describe different areas of consulting you provide, so the client can pull out one or two sections that are appropriate to their needs.

Often, clients get busy and don't call consultants back when they say they will (imagine that!). So, we have to make a judgment call about the appropriate length of time to circle back and make that call ourselves. We want to demonstrate that we're interested in working with the company without feeling like we're harassing the client with uninvited phone calls.

Why not let your current satisfied clients help you out? One way to do this is to ask the (potential) client, "When would you like for me to get back in touch with you?" Established clients can provide testimonials to potential clients, either by phone, email or letter, as a follow up to your sales call. If you have a solid relationship with a client, she is likely to be happy to send a short note recommending you, as long as you don't abuse this by asking for testimonials every day.

At the beginning of this chapter, we inserted a line from a movie—"Always be selling." We put that in the book because we believe that we are always selling, whether it's consciously or not. We'd prefer to be intentional. For instance, we have what we call our "elevator speech" that succinctly describes what we do in the event we meet someone in an elevator who asks us, "So, what do you do?" We have a fifteen-second one in case it's a short elevator ride and a slightly longer one in case it's a high rise. Linda's short pitch is: "I help organizations leverage the talents of their diverse workforce so the company can grow and thrive in a global society." Short, to the point, and accurate!

I was in Memphis, on a Hertz shuttle bus on the way to the airport. I'd had a full couple of days with a client and was still energized from a successful visit. Three gentlemen in the seat across the aisle were discussing protective labor laws around training and development. They were puzzled about how to apply these regulations in their workplace. We had a seven-minute ride to the airport, so I jumped in when there was a pause and said that I couldn't help overhearing their conversation (of course not, they were one foot away from me). I let them know what I do as a consultant and shared the correct way to implement the protective labor law they were discussing. They were very appreciative and mentioned the name of their company, which was near where I live. I told them I lived nearby, and that I was on my way home to Cincinnati. So were they! The more senior of the group asked if he could see if he could switch seats so he could sit next to me on the plane and ask me a few more questions about my work and how I might be able to help them on a consulting basis—they're still a client today.

Terri

Whatever your goal, your first priority is to address two daunting thoughts:

1. You have to make money in order to survive; and

2. How much money you make depends on you now.

As I mentioned in an earlier chapter, I was absolutely spoiled on my first sales call. The prospect responded to our discussion by saying, "I didn't know there were people out there like you."[vii] I got the contract. I still didn't have any confidence in my ability to sell, but at least I had a positive experience and was willing to try again.

That first sales opportunity came from networking, so I reasoned that networking was the way to sales. However, as I learned along the way, you can starve if you wait for people to remember you and remember to recommend you.

You do have to remind them. You do have to ask them to refer you. You do have to ask for testimonials. Of course, the best way to remind people is in person, the second best is using the phone, the third is a letter or email. Many people I know jump right to email because it is the easiest. However, it is not the most effective. You may have known that already.

"The woman that deliberates is lost."
—Joseph Addison (1672–1719), British essayist

Sales has been the most difficult business concept for me to embrace. Therefore, I make it a practice to document the sales "lessons" I learn as I continue my consulting journey. The following lessons are ones that I have incorporated into my sales beliefs.

SALES TENETS

1. You don't have a business until you have a client.
2. Getting a client requires you to sell *yourself*.

vii Thank you, Bob Brewster.

3. The purpose of the first meeting is to make certain there is a second.
4. If people don't like you, they won't hire you.
5. If people don't trust you, you will not get a contract.
6. If you don't deliver with quality, on time and on budget, you will not get a second contract.
7. They have to hurt, they have to need you, they have to want what you have to offer, and the timing has to be right—no hurt, no need, no help, no hurry.

But guidelines are like policies—they only apply 98 percent of the time. There is always room for an exception. Some rare individual CEOs indicate they aren't in a "hurry" and actually want to be proactive and hire you to do an assessment. If they do, these individuals usually have recently taken over the firm, either from family or by purchase. These clients view this as a rare opportunity to assess their needs in a strategic, long-term way and to identify those areas where you may be able to help the firm. On the other hand, I have seen numerous large company managers conduct an assessment so that they can check-off-the-box on the list of things the CEO wanted them to do. The assessment is placed on the top shelf of the supply closet—in the back.

Normally, when I receive a phone call, the organization is experiencing pain and seeking to relieve it. The CEO is frequently in a hurry because the problem was either not recognized or has been stewing and wasn't handled earlier in a timely way. In this case, they need speed—a quick solution. A simple solution. If you can't resolve the situation immediately, then they don't need you. This is not the time for in-depth study. This is problem-solving time.

Let me share a story with you I tell sometimes to prospects when they ask why they should use my firm.

A small business CEO is distracted by the problems at the company. As CEO Pat Smart crosses the street toward her business, she does not notice the deep hole in the road. She falls into the hole. After finding that nothing is broken, she gets up dusts herself off and begins to call from her hole in the ground to passersby for help.

A consultant with a "Big Six" firm walks by and she calls to him, "Please help me!" The man says, "Of course, I will help you. Let me get on my cell phone and give the office a call. I will have the best and brightest of our new young associates come out and study the situation and give you a report on how best to get out of that hole. By the way, our minimum fee is $50,000 for this type of study."

And, off he goes.

A lawyer walks by and Pat calls to him "Please help me. I have fallen into this hole and I can't get out!"

"No problem," says the lawyer. "I think we have a liability claim against the city for not covering this hole! I will get the paperwork started right away. Here is my card. Give me a call and I think we may have a multimillion dollar suit on our hands. Don't forget to call me." He tosses down his card and walks away.

Frustrated, the CEO has little choice but to call out to the next person who walks by. "Please help me!" Pat Smart calls to the woman walking by.

The woman jumps down in the hole.

"What are you doing?" Pat cries out, "now, we're both stuck!"

"Don't worry," says the consultant from Just The Basics®, "I have been here before and I know the way out."

Just The Basics®
Vital Business Results
Proudly serving small businesses for over seventeen years.

This is problem solving at its best. If you are successful in resolving the pain to their satisfaction, then you may have an opportunity to work more proactively in the future.

WHAT WE SELL

When we sell consulting, we are selling ourselves. We may offer our time, expertise, and perspective in one of three "basic" categories: problem solving, continuous improvement, and innovation. A brief description of problem solving, continuous improvement and innovation follows.

Terri

PROBLEM-SOLVING, CONTINUOUS IMPROVEMENT AND INNOVATION

When I began my practice, I had been a problem-solver for over twenty years, and an expert in continuous improvement for ten. I have studied and taught innovation over the past ten years. I have used each of these concepts in my own practice as well as with clients; where possible, I use new concepts within my own firm first, before rolling out any new concept to my clients. Unless clients understand and volunteer for a new model, I don't use it unless we both understand what the concept entails and what the risks are to taking a new and different approach.

Problem solving is the most rewarded management activity and requires that the individual move the organization out of a problem and back to the status quo. If this is the first time the client has encountered the problem, then a quick fix and return to the status quo may be in order. If the problem has occurred more than once, it may be time for the client to consider either a continuous improvement effort, or an innovative solution.

Continuous improvement is taking mundane everyday tasks and creating small measured steps toward improvements in processes and procedures. This may be a much less rewarded activity, but over time can make significant improvements in a company and decrease operating costs. Like compound interest, a simple one percent improvement per day, per week or per month compounds into truly substantial changes.

Here's an example of how I incorporated problem solving and continuous improvement in one project.

> The problem was the workflow of a particular procedure in my client's garment manufacturing business. We began by analyzing one sub process of the client's workflow. This effort took four hours charting and talking with the four employees involved in the process of tagging garments through the garment construction process. The cost of the time for the consultant, the owner, and all four employees totaled X dollars. The employees identified both the current process and the problems, and then we identified solutions and charted those. The cost savings to the client was 2X dollar annually —both an immediate and recurring savings based on a half-day of continuous improvement work.
>
> Application: The approach to the problem we solved was low-tech - drawing boxes filled with text , on flip-chart paper posted around the walls. The most high tech tools of the exercise were the colored markers. Rather than take the time to remove the charts from the walls and document them immediately in the procedures notebook, the client left the charts on the walls so that everyone would see them (and be reminded) every day for six months. By choosing this approach, the client reinforced the new process without any other reminders, and in six months, the charts were translated to the procedures book for new employees. The current employees had already incorporated the new process from the daily reminder of the posted charts. They weren't pretty, they weren't high tech, but they provided the necessary process reinforcement that had been designed by the employees.

On the other hand, innovation requires an organization to create a work environment that rewards failure as a step toward success. Innovation appears to thrive in an environment where there is a rush-to-market, creating laser focus, and where the product or service disrupts the marketplace (Procter and Gamble's dry floor mop, Swiffer, for example), and/or in an environment where good enough is good enough. Where this environment exists, the product or service doesn't continue in this "good enough" status; instead, improvements continue until the offering moves from simply functional to convenient, reliable and cost-effective. Importantly, then work begins again to disrupt the product of service just introduced. (Think Procter and Gamble's Swiffer, then Swiffer Wet Jet, and then . . . you get the idea). Some work environments are designed that way, as in the skunk works of many technology-based industries, such as aerospace and technology; other companies have to change the "fabric" of the organization so that innovation can take place.

Every work environment is a different culture and requires a different approach.

Teaching innovation[47] helped me to identify the basic components of innovation and apply them to the sales process, as well as the consulting process. First, disrupt the status quo with your introduction. Then, address the essential components with your new product or service, as follows:

1. Functionality—Can it work? Does it work?
2. Convenience—Is it easy to access? Is it easy to use?
3. Cost—What is the value of the product? (Hint: First to Market as well as New and Improved, as trite as they may be, still justify the higher pricing.)
4. Reliability—Will you be there when they need you? Is the product or service reliable?

RELATIONSHIPS

There is a contemporary theory that a consultant shouldn't become too close to clients for fear that the consultant will lose their objectivity. If that were true, then no one inside an organization would be of value for very long—they would be tainted by the closeness that comes from getting to know their own clients, the employees and the operations well.

My sales philosophy was garnered from Jim Moon, a retired flavorist from Fries and Fries, Tastemaker and Givaudan. He was not a sales person, but a technical genius when it came to making alcoholic beverage flavors —the only person I knew that had the distinguished title of Vice President, Alcoholic Beverages. He used to tell me that "If you make your customer your friend, and you lose a customer, you still have a friend." Thanks to Jim, that has become my sales philosophy.

There is a fine edge in selling, which I consider an art. You can't appear to want the sale so much that you're anxious, even if you don't know where the mortgage money is coming from next month. And, you can't appear too confident, or the prospect thinks you don't care. I have done both, with disastrous effects. True, there are times when I did need the money, and there were times when I didn't need the work (or the check), but the client wants to know that you're there for them and not yourself. Focusing entirely on the prospect and their needs is the only way to sell your services.

I won't tell you that I am an accomplished salesperson; I'm not. If I like the potential client, then I am prone to give away too much and actually begin consulting during the sales process.

Being conscious of what you are giving away is key to your successful sales practices, and I am still working on this one.

If I don't particularly like the client, I walk away or recommend another consultant. However, I also recommend other consultants if I believe they would do a better job on this type of assignment.

Linda

SPECIAL SALES OPPORTUNITIES

We'd like to touch on two other sales opportunities: sales that flow from publications, and sales that flow from conferences and presentations. If you like to write, we hope you'll consider this avenue to open doors for your consulting practice. If you enjoy public speaking and training, this is yet another sales opportunity. Linda has written three books prior to this one, and each has generated not only book sales, but sales in consulting contracts as well. During conference presentations, consultants are asked to discuss topics on which they're expert. It's important to keep in mind this opportunity is intended to help consultants present themselves in a positive light in front of potential clients, *not* as a forum for making an overt sales pitch. If you do an excellent job presenting your ideas, people will come up afterwards and ask for your card. Many will actually follow up and invite you to make a sales call. Some conference committees will provide speakers with an attendee list. Unless after-conference contact by speakers is prohibited in the contract, this is a chance to follow up with people who attended your session with a thank-you note, and an article that provides more information on the topic.

Terri

PROPOSALS AND HANDSHAKES

Most of my contracts in the early years were handshake agreements. My paternal grandfather used to say, "If a man is not as good as his handshake, then no contract is going to make that better."

If the client didn't ask for a contract, a proposal, or a written report, they didn't get one. My small business clients appreciated the fact that they weren't going to be charged for a written report when all they wanted was to hear the results of my analysis. A written report was a waste of my time and their money.

As for proposals and contracts, when my projects became more complex or when there was more than just the CEO involved, it became necessary to put more information in writing. This included the results that a client hoped to achieve, plus the products and services Just The Basics® would provide, and a timeline for delivery.

As larger organizations became clients, it became necessary to gather additional details since more people were involved in expressing expectations, and/or one or both of us anticipated project scope changes. The bigger the project, the more likely that there was room for misunderstanding. Writing down the expectations for both the client and the consultant simply added clarification.

Eventually, I was advised to at least have a letter of agreement. Then, my attorney suggested that I might want to get the client signature on the letter of agreement and I started doing that. Then, my banker wanted an expansion of the letter of agreement to signed contracts. Normally, I followed the counsel of my advisors. They did not make suggestions in a vacuum. I knew they have my best interest at heart and suggested only those items of benefit to all concerned. That being said, for some of my more established clients, when I am certain that we understand each other, a handshake is still good enough for me.

My guidelines:

1. If the project involves a sub-contractor, then the project is big enough for a proposal and a signed contract.
2. If the project involves more than the CEO, then the project is complex enough for a proposal and a signed contract.

3. If the project involves the board of directors, or will be presented to a board of directors, then the project requires a proposal and a signed contract.

SALES CONSULTANT ADVICE

Just as I hope that prospects will ask for help in my area of expertise, I also recognize when I need help. Since I am not an excellent salesperson, I hired a sales coach, Pam Beigh, from SalesScore. I saw results immediately. I learned it was important for me to ask my prospective client three questions:

1. What would you like from me next?
2. When would you like for me to follow-up with you?
3. What is your decision process on this project?

These recommendations were exactly on target and helped me to get "unstuck" as I improved my sales skills.

Linda

SUMMARY

We're often asked by new consultants about the percentage of time we spend prospecting, making cold calls, and preparing marketing materials. We could easily spend all of our time with any one or all of these activities and not ever get around to consulting! We know consultants who've fallen into that trap, and we don't want that to happen to you.

I spend no time—that's zero time—on cold calls or blanket mailers about my services. That's a choice I made early on because I simply don't enjoy this type of activity, so I know I won't excel in this area. Once a year, I take a brutally honest look at my web site and determine where it needs updating. Then I write the updates required to send to my (wonderful!) website guru. This takes about eight hours of my time. The return on investment is many times this eight hours since the website is one of my primary marketing methods.

I update my brochure at the same time I update the website, and that takes about an hour. Remember, though, that I've been at this for twenty years now. When I first developed my website, I easily invested forty hours over a month-long period of time and my initial brochure took another ten hours. My motto is "do it right the first time and avoid constant rewrites!"

erri

Linda's comments on "doing it right the first time" certainly rings true to me. My first website was developed in 1995, and has undergone two major revisions plus annual updates since then. In general, I spend approximately 25 percent of my time marketing and selling, with networking as the first step in the process. While this time investment ebbs and flows, it has not changed significantly since the third year of my business; during the first two years, I spent 50 percent of my time on those activities.

9

Keep It Coming! Cash Flow

Terri

A plethora of information is available about cash flow and how critical it is to any business, but how well we remember our early teachings has a strong impact on how we manage our finances.

When my dad first went into business for himself in 1949, he had a business partner. Dad's partner, Daryl, handled all the paperwork and the accounts receivable. On Saturday mornings, Daryl would go to the homes of their customers to collect the money for the work performed throughout the week. If the person said he did not have the money, Daryl would say, "If you don't pay me, my kids don't eat this week." And, he continued to stand there on the porch. He got the money.

When Dad bought out his partner a few years later, he didn't follow Daryl's collection practice and cash flow slowed down, but eventually past due bills were collected. If a customer was over sixty-five and on a fixed income or didn't have the money, Dad would collect the cost of the materials and not charge any labor. He could not bear for anyone to have a broken pipe or not have heat.

The cash flow may have slowed, but the money was nearly always collected.

~

However, nothing teaches us better than our own experience. My first experience came when I was twenty-five years old.

The year was 1974, when Richard Nixon was forced to resign, inflation raged at 11.3 percent, and the prime interest rate was 12 percent; I was twenty-four. I could do anything. My world was me, my career, and my boyfriend. I wanted to complete my undergraduate degree—I needed the degree to climb the career ladder.

But, I couldn't afford to return to college. I had a job making $7,500 a year when the national average was $13,900; but that worked out to be $1.60 more per hour than the national minimum wage of $2.00. I thought I was doing OK for someone without a degree.

My monthly income of $625 was being used for:

Mandatory tax withholdings and benefits: $125

Apartment: $100

Car payment: $90

Utilities: $70

Gas: 55 cents per gallon

Parking: $22

Lunches out: $44

Groceries: $125

Those expenditures left less than $20 per month for anything else, including recreation (and remember I was only twenty-four). So, I cut back—two or more days a week I took the bus and packed my lunch. I didn't eat out, but cooked at home each night.

If I wanted to return to school, I had to do something more drastic.

Here was my plan:

1. Negotiate my full-time salaried job to part-time hourly status.
2. Move to a third floor walk-up apartment at $65 per month with no air conditioning.
3. Buy used textbooks.
4. Eat lots of peanut butter and jelly sandwiches.
5. Sell the car to make the tuition payment (I could take the bus free because I worked for the bus company).
6. Take the bus from my University of Cincinnati apartment location to downtown for work, then to Northern Kentucky University to go to school.

As a result, I had a lower rent payment, fewer utility costs (especially without air conditioning), no car payment, no gasoline charges, no parking fees, and no bus fare). And, no time for recreation with a full class load of fifteen hours and a part-time job that averaged thirty-seven and half hours a week over the course of that year.

That is a cash flow problem with a happy ending—a degree and a $3,000 raise when I finished the degree.

I faced my second cash flow learning experience less than ten years later. By 1978, my boyfriend, De, had become my husband and he wanted to start a business—he asked me to sign the papers pledging all our assets to fund the business. Our joint assets at the time amounted to two used cars and a house we had purchased on a land contract in 1975. Not a lot of equity there, but the bank found it symbolic of our commitment and by then I had improved my earnings capacity and was "upwardly mobile." My husband had a partner, Druce, who was the husband of my best friend. The four of us signed away our lives. Our husbands would work the business full-time, but if my friend, Marita, and I were going to pledge the collateral, including our future salaries and our homes, then we were going to be involved in the business. Marita and I each worked two full-time jobs: first our day-jobs, then nights and weekends at the new business.

The business was a ground-floor operation, actually, bare walls—a frame shop and photo studio. We grew that business by finding a niche in the corporate framing market that was virtually untapped at the time. Photo shoots in the food and fashion business, as well as portraits were the basis of the photo operation. Druce turned the bare walls into a small art gallery, focusing on local artists. Then we purchased a photo processing laboratory in downtown Cincinnati. Now, we had two locations to manage.

Along with that happy business success story, the rest of the tale is this: at one point, we had a new baby, bought a new house, and couldn't sell the old one. We had two mortgages on both houses and the expense of a new baby. Our small business was not yet making a profit. That makes me stressed (even now) just thinking about it. Then, the company I worked for merged and I didn't have a job.

That is called a cash flow problem.

Eventually, the business became profitable, and after five years of building two businesses, we decided to sell. As outlined in our original Buy-Sell agreement, our partners bought the business and subsequently sold it as three businesses. We were proud that we had created three businesses and ten jobs out of one start-up in just under five years. It's true that small businesses are the economic engine of our country and the creators of net new jobs. (Remember the numbers in Chapter Two about 80 percent of the jobs surviving even when the businesses did not? This is a good example of how that works.) Statistically, the business didn't survive, but it did morph into three businesses with ten employees. The employees continued to have jobs after the sale.

The rest of the story is I got a new job. After fifteen months, we sold the first house and paid off the two mortgages on it; it took another five years to pay off the second mortgage on the second house.

What lessons did I learn about cash flow? I learned that business is fraught with risks and the only way to manage that risk is to believe in yourself and those around you to do the best that they can all the time. I believed then (and still believe) that if you do the right thing—supply value with the services you provide —that everything will work out for the best. I also learned to create a little cushion when the money comes in to save for a rainy day. Later I took this knowledge into my own business and I learned to balance my portfolio of clients and services so that there was a more steady flow of work. Two lessons I learned in creating a steady flow of work and cash were: 1) not worrying about how to manage the time it takes to complete a project until you have the project and 2) propose more work than you can handle. While I was successful in ninety percent of attempts to get the business, the project start date was usually postponed from the original request date.

The other lesson I learned (over time) was that small businesses and nonprofits were on a different time scale—in other words, the economy dictated (to some degree) which type of organization was most likely to have needs. Each business owner has to determine these patterns for herself and make certain that the services provided have a time frame that matches her needs. Another example of this lesson learned was a pattern to the services requested—one year, revised compensation plans were all the rage, another year it was employee handbooks, another strategic plans. I didn't understand the drivers for these patterns, but I learned to welcome them just the same.

PROFITS ARE NOT CASH FLOW

During the first five years of my consulting business, I learned that profits are not cash flow. There has to be cash coming in regularly to keep your business afloat. How you bill your clients, how you collect your money, and when you collect your money are important to your business success. Bill early and collect promptly.

The flow of money is just as important as earning it. My clients were billed at the end of the project or the month, depending upon the arrangement. That meant, even if they paid within thirty days, I could have eighty-nine days of accounts receivable outstanding. (For example, it's January 2, work begins and you purchase needed supplies for the project, you expend your labor on one client so that it can't be spent on another client or sales activities; the project is scheduled for February 15th delivery. You bill at the end of February; the client pays at the end of March.)

Time for changes. With a business in its early years, people may not want to pay you in advance; however, I offer a discount for prepayment of the total amount of the project. Established clients frequently take me up on this offer. For new clients, if the project is to last over thirty days, then I bill at the end of the thirty days, even if it is mid-month. For me what works today is either total prepayment, or payment in three segments; one-third up-front and two equal installments at the next thirty-day intervals.

Most small business owners understand cash flow well and will agree to a ten-day turn around on invoices. You can bill at the end of the month in which the work completed or if the project is completed on the fifteenth, you can bill on the sixteenth. Little steps, baby steps really, but every day that your money is outstanding, someone else is using it.

In 1998, I took out a line of credit at a local bank to handle the cash flow issues, but that was secured by the equity in my home. It cost a lot of interest money that year and the up-front fee seemed expensive. I decided that I had to do something differently for the future, so that I wouldn't have to take out a line of credit in the future. (That would change.)

That cash flow education was expensive, but worth it. My philosophy regarding money was engrained, and I decided to re-embrace these principles:

- Do a good job—an excellent job—and the money will be there.
- You want your clients to trust you and so you must trust them.

Childhood memories can have a strong impact on us. Here's my second childhood remembrance about client trust and cash flow; it's one of my favorite stories about my dad, my mom, and money.

Terri

Mom and Dad were working in their retail plumbing shop one Saturday morning when a man came in and asked for some plumbing parts. Dad went back into the shop and got them for him, brought them out, and began writing up the receipt.

The customer said, "Cliff, I don't have the money today, but I will bring it to you next Saturday."

My Dad smiled and said, "I'll be here." and the man left with the parts.

Dad turned to Mom and said "Delores, who was that?"

Mom said, "Cliff, I don't know."

They both laughed. Mom filed the sales slip without a name on it and the day went on.

The next Saturday, the man with the unknown name, returned and paid the bill. To this day, no one knows the name of that man.

Balancing the concepts from both my childhood and my own experience has always been a challenge, but I learned:

- If you want trust, you have to give it.
- If you want your money, you have to ask for it.
- If your client can't afford to pay and you want to do the work, you can find a way.

I trust my clients to do what they say they will do. Occasionally, one of them doesn't. However, they always pay what they agreed to pay. I have never failed to collect a fee, even when my banker has advised me to write it off. It is a matter of principle—the client received the work and the contract—handshake or written, and that means I receive the compensation I am due.

Occasionally you have to ask multiple times to receive your money (keep in mind, that early in my practice, I did things differently than I do now). My suggestion is to call five days after a payment is due, and again (if necessary) after thirty days. At sixty days, I have been known to send a payment reminder with an interest charge. After that, I call every week until I receive a check. I once had a client that paid after 120 days, but that was the only time I experienced such a delay in payment.

Under the category of finding a way to offer services without payment, I offer a discounted rate to nonprofits and give five, free local presentations each year. A couple of them are standing commitments. Some are presentations for graduate and undergraduate classes, the others are usually association speaking engagements where there isn't a speaker budget. If the associations have a small budget, I sometimes ask them to donate an honorarium to my favorite charity. Unfortunately, I cannot always accommodate all the requests, but I do make a commitment to provide free presentations five times per year.

A woman in one of those free presentation audiences, during the Q and A session stated "I have been told that relationships are one of the things that you have to pay attention to in consulting. What do you think?" I responded, "Relationships are not 'one of the things' in business, they are the only thing."

nda

Terri and I agree on many aspects of consulting, and this last statement is one that I am unbending on as well. There is no question in my mind that the reason I've been in business for twenty years is because of the carefully nurtured relationships I've developed.

There have been times through the years that I've done work for free to support a growing relationship with a client or colleague. There have been times when I've gone out of my way to do extra research, or introduce a client to someone who could assist them—all to support a growing relationship. I believe it's part of the Karma "thing"—what you send out into the universe comes back to you, many times over.

Even though I've built and nurtured relationships out of friendship and because the people involved were interesting, there have been many times when I've ended up with new clients . . . long-term clients. My client Michelle is one example that springs to mind immediately. In the mid-nineties, I taught in the graduate program of Labor and Employment Relations at the University of Cincinnati. One of the courses I taught was Managing Workplace Diversity. Michelle sat in the front row, by the window. She was a bright light in that class, with her insightful comments and questions. Over the years, she has grown personally and professionally to a point where I now go to her for advice and recommendations!

Here's another instance about the benefits of building relationships. About eight years ago, I was at my desk working on a project and a young woman called me who was interested in moving from the accounting profession into human resources. Someone had referred her to me for an informational interview because that had been my career path. I don't remember talking with her because so many people call me with similar questions and requests for advice. Last summer, however, this young woman surfaced in my life again. I was responding to a Request for Proposal for a large utility company in Cincinnati for a substantial project. While I was making a presentation in front of a selection team, there was a young woman on the team who was very friendly and asked questions that definitely set me up for success. Once I had the project, she popped up again as a participant in one of the workshops I was presenting for the company. I walked up to her and asked if we'd ever met. She smiled and told me that I had taken a great deal of time with her over the phone many years ago, helping her decide whether HR was for her. She had been encouraged and helped by my advice. She remembered that day, and when she saw that I was bidding on the project, she was highly instrumental in my selection. There's that Karma "thing" again.

Our society is global. That means that our competitors, vendors, colleagues—and customers—come from many cultures from around the world. Other cultures outside the U.S., such as in Southeast Asia, are very relationship oriented. I discovered when I lived in Japan that nobody gets awarded business contracts immediately. The process is lengthy, and the purchaser of goods and services wants to know the people with whom they're dealing with on a personal level. Whether you naturally gravitate toward building relationships in the business world—or not—this is a competency we both encourage you to develop. The results are well worth the effort.

LESSONS LEARNED

The primary keys to positive cash flow are good relationships, trust in people, and timely billing.

Cash flow does not equal profits. If you don't manage cash flow, you can find yourself borrowing money on which to operate, costing you interest charges. Even worse, you could end up with a poor credit score if you fail to repay a loan on time. Borrowing money costs money—money you can keep if you improve cash flow.

The money you earn is yours—it is not someone else's money. Collecting money owed to you is an important milestone in managing your project—you wouldn't leave a project incomplete would you?

10

The Best Clients for Women

Terri

What's so different about being a woman consultant? I don't hear the question as often as I see it in people's eyes.

The practice of consulting does not change with gender. I am not suggesting that men and women do not consult differently—I believe they do, but I don't view the variance as much due to gender as I do to other factors, such as personality style, work orientation, or a myriad of other factors.

This book is intended to outline those ideas about running a consulting business that may be unique to women. The things I mention may not be universal, but they are my experiences and I get the question just often enough to want to share the answers more broadly.

First, adapting to the consultant's world when you are "on your own" is very different from adapting to a male culture in a corporation—it takes about 30 percent less energy and time. You make a few critical decisions early in your practice, such as how you are going to operate this business.

You will base your operating philosophy on proven business principles and your own values. Your values, intentions, principles, and vision of the "right way" to run a business, all form the basis of your business operations. Then, only once a season or so, do you face new decisions, like cleaning out your closet—keep them, throw them away, modify them. My philosophies and beliefs have remained constant, and there is a cost of doing business this way, which I will describe, but the value far outweighs the cost.

CHANGING CLOTHES THREE TIMES A DAY.

Really? Corporate attire is not what my clients want to see, with one exception, whom I can tell prefers that I wear a corporate suit—preferably a skirt. (This particular CEO, a male, is not sexist—I have never heard a word from him or observed any other behavior that could remotely be misinterpreted.) However, even though this CEO wears jeans to the office nearly every day, he wants his advisors to be—and look—the same in dealing with him as if they were consulting with a Fortune 500 corporate officer. How can I tell?—the results of our meetings. When I am "power attired" I observe that he listens better—he wants to actively engage in discussions that involve both the pros and cons of what he is considering, and needs less data to back up his decisions. When I have appeared in more casual attire (as in going from a meeting with an informal client to his office) my effectiveness is diminished.

On the other hand—tech companies like informality and appear to distrust people who dress in a corporate way. A friend once advised that you cannot deduct the cost of clothing on your tax return until you have come up with a "consultant's uniform." I have given serious thought to that concept.

Interestingly, my volunteer service on local boards requires me to dress up more than my small business clients. Again, it seems to be for the same reason as my blue-jeans client: it's the perception of expertise that accompanies the "suited attire." Therefore, depending upon my schedule for the day, especially those days that require a 7 AM to 8PM schedule, I may change clothes three times a day to be what I believe is the most effective. Men would just remove their jacket and tie. I have only recently found a look that works in nearly all environments. Changing clothes three times a day takes its toll—comfortable casual for meeting a colleague for breakfast—change clothes—corporate attire for lunch board meeting, and then change clothes - business casual attire for the afternoon with a client. Then, I may have to change for an evening appointment. That lasted for a few years until I figured out how much time I spent changing clothes—and that was eating into my billable time.

THE BEST CLIENTS FOR WOMEN

April 13, 2006 Woman to Woman

As I drove to my client's office, through the streets of downtown, the traffic lights went out and I traveled the last two miles, one block at a time, slinking through the intersections in case other drivers didn't take turns, as they were supposed to do.

When I arrived at the retail shop, the lights were out—it was daytime, so it was not apparent until I walked inside. The owner unlocked the door, since we always met prior to her opening the store to her customers. Her production employees were already working and, obviously being very distracted by the lack of light. The chaos that reigned was too much for any of us to concentrate.

She owned the place next door, where the sunshine streamed into the front retail window, and where a comfortable living room was set for display. By the light of only the morning sunshine, we sat there

> for hours, talking and going over the documents from our last meeting. I felt like a mannequin in a movie set. All the shop owners, bankers, and restaurateurs were out roaming the streets. There was no coffee to be had, no sales to be facilitated, no dollars to be exchanged; the stores were all closed because there was no electricity.
>
> Just two women sitting in the window of a closed shop, talking, laughing, moving the business forward on a different level—the planning one —which would more than make up for the three hours of lost client traffic for her business.

The best clients for women are those who:

- Prefer women consultants, or
- Don't have a gender preference; they only want the best consultant for the job.

I have never had a potential client say or indicate in any way, "Oh, I didn't know you were a woman. I want to work with a man." On the other hand, I have had male and female clients say, "I like working with you. Sometimes it is just easier to talk to a woman."

Good consultants get new work through referrals, so your reputation and gender precede you. If someone doesn't want to work with a woman, you won't receive the call in the first place.

In HR consulting, since half of the professionals are women, it is seldom an issue. When clients hurt and they are seeking help, the fact that you are female is of little consequence to the client. They just want their problem solved and the pain to go away.

MAIL, PHONE AND INTERNET CLIENTS

For six years, I didn't hear one work from a particular client, and then I received a phone call from him: he had a problem and needed advice on an employee relations issue. I gave the advice (which I would not have been able to do, if they had not been a client previously), sent an invoice, and got paid. The following year, the same client called and wanted me to update their employee handbook, then e-mailed it to me. I proposed changes, had them approved and sent a final document along with an invoice, which was promptly paid. For the past five years, I have provided services via phone and email only for this client. They have moved into larger facilities twice since I began working with them. I haven't seen the last two locations. But their business has continued to grow and develop in the same field, with the same type of employees. I know the HR business and I know *their* business.

Fewer on-site meetings are the norm now, a significant change from the beginning of my consulting business. More email, more phone calls, and less mail by regular delivery and nearly always by courier or express delivery services. It's not a matter of money, but convenience. My work is done in a seventy-five-mile radius of downtown Cincinnati, Ohio. I don't charge for travel time, and if the client is within twenty-five miles, I also don't charge for mileage. Therefore, convenience is a primary factor, not money, since the price is the same whether I travel or don't. But, no travel is less expensive and saves time.

Also, I maintain a membership in a city club for the convenience of my clients (and for me). If my clients want to meet away from their operating facility, with or without me, I offer them the opportunity to meet at my city club —in the restaurant, the library or a private meeting room.

BEST CLIENT PROFILES

My best clients are profiled below along with the reasons I consider them the best under client common denominators. I consider all of my clients as unique and special and some will meet the common denominator criteria. However, our book is not a client profile book and we have only a chapter to devote to best clients. We have each chosen three that represent the many of which we are extremely fond.

Small Business

My first small business client was Industrial Paint & Supply, a coating solutions company that offers corrosion control coatings for industrial applications. In 1995, the owners had had the business for less than two years. Since that time, we have grown together. They have grown from five employees to ten, expanded their facilities from 1,700 square feet to 9,000 square feet of operations, and increased revenue from a $800,000 to $3 million. The owner, George Berry, and his son, Marty Berry, began this partnership together; Marty has now taken over the business.

What makes Marty Berry a particular joy and a pleasure to work with is his unbridled enthusiasm, and his commitment to his employees and to his business. He pays at or above market rate in wages and salaries, offers good benefits, and works to develop his employees, offering as much training as the employees can manage to integrate into the business schedule each year. Marty offers just enough structure to provide comfort to employees—the boundaries, such as job descriptions; an employee handbook, which he updates regularly; and regularly-scheduled formal performance reviews.

This is an employer who provides words of praise or small gifts as recognition for effort and gives bonus rewards for results; he has picnics in the summer and holiday parties to develop camaraderie among the employees.

He manages to balance his life between his two active teenagers and the business by delegating as much as possible to his employees. Marty is a hands-on manager who works in the operation—not an absentee owner, but he "let's go" of the things others can do in the business.

Prior to his experience as a business owner, he had been a computer programmer with a small independent service business (without employees) for maintaining yachts in Hawaii.

In 1995, he hired me to help with the resolution of an employee embezzlement problem and to learn how to hire great performing and trustworthy employees. We've worked together every year since that time, taking the organization to the next appropriate level as he has grown. I say "we," because I feel as though I am a partner in his business. Marty has done a remarkable job in getting my "discretionary energy" devoted to his business. Discretionary energy is like the change in your pocket—the little extra amount you save so that you can give it to something you care about. This discretionary energy may not be much on a given day, but over time, it can add up quite significantly. (Try putting all of your pocket change in a jar for just one week.) Discretionary energy should be devoted to something of value—I use my discretionary energy when I create ideas on how to better build or manage my clients' businesses. This is free "strategic thinking time" from an outsider's perspective; no matter how much time I spend "brainstorming" within my own head, I don't send a bill for this time. There are a limited number of clients I know well enough, and fewer still that inspire me, to devote this type of my time to their concerns.

Nonprofit

Fort Hamilton Healthcare Corporation is a healthcare umbrella corporation with two retirement facilities as well as a private dining club, daycare facility, school, foundation, wellness center, community behavior services, and community pharmacy. I did my first work for this client in one of the retirement facilities, Westover Senior Services, in 1996. We completed a management compensation plan and an employee communications plan; and I coached the HR manager.

In 1998, the two retirement facilities, Westover Senior Services and Colonial Senior Services, merged under the Fort Hamilton Healthcare umbrella, resulting in one operating entity named Colonial Senior Services. From 1998 to 2001, I provided Colonial with services focusing on the integration of the two retirement facilities, along with the Colonial Foundation and preschool. Additionally, I provided executive coaching.

Six years later, the former president of Colonial Services, Jeff Thurman, became president of the Fort Hamilton Healthcare Corporation. His board had requested a proposal for an executive compensation plan; Jeff remembered our work together a few years earlier and asked me to provide a proposal. His board was comfortable with the proposal and I began a six-month project resulting in a compensation plan for the executive team. Previously, I had had the opportunity to work with Jeff's staff. Now, I had the opportunity to work with his executive staff and his board on the compensation project.

This is a CEO and a nonprofit organization that values employees as well as the business end of the operations. Jeff manages a diverse, multiple-entity organization that is comparable to a multi-division private corporation. He seeks superior talent for his executive team, delegates work, is good to his employees, and manages his board appropriately. He knows the business and is an integral part of the community in which he lives and works. Community leaders seek his advice before proceeding with unrelated community development activities.

Small Business

The name of the third company will remain anonymous, for reasons that will become obvious. This woman owned firm employs a majority of individuals who have ADD[viii]– attention deficit disorder. This was not

viii Also referred to as ADHD, attention deficit hyperactive disorder. For more information, read *Delivered From Distraction*, by Edward M. Hallowell, M.D. and John J. Ratey, M.D.

her original intention; however, she had friends who shared this disorder. This unusual staffing became apparent as I worked with her firm. When I asked her about this, she replied that she thought this was true, and while these individuals were more of a challenge to manage, they were also the most creative individuals that she had interviewed. "If they remain on their medication", she said, "they are the most productive employees as well." She went on to explain that other employers overlooked these individuals as too difficult to manage, but "I have experience and I get the most talented and creative people by just realizing they have a disability and knowing how to deal with that." "You know," she said, "they are not ADD; they have ADD."

I have observed her employees think outside the box and problem-solve with great success. I have watched as she managed the difficult days and I have been amazed at the productivity of her small firm. I am always impressed.

I have provided these profiles because these clients possess what I call "Best Client Common Denominators."

BEST CLIENT COMMON DENOMINATORS

What is the common denominator among the clients that are best for Just The Basics®? Perhaps it boils down to values, intent and courage.

The best leaders of the best organizations have solid values that they adhere to in the worst of times, as well as the best of times. They value individual employees, they value their customers, they value home and family, they value the business of their businesses, and they seek a balance that works.

Their intent is pure. They want to do the right thing, at the right time, in the right way. Their intention is to do that. Are they always successful?

No. They are human beings with sometimes wrenchingly conflicting goals, or incorrect or missing data at the time a decision is made. The important thing to me, is that their intention is to do the right thing and they act accordingly.

They possess the courage to do the right thing. They are willing to make hard decisions when necessary. They address unproductive and disruptive employees appropriately. They discuss with their investors, both emotional and financial investors, the right way to do things. When it comes down to crunch time, they can and do make the unpopular or difficult decision. They know when to say "no" and they say no. They know when to say "yes" and they say yes. They have the courage of their convictions; they take responsibility for their decisions, and the decisions of those who report to them. They take the harder right way instead of the easier way.

Because of these attributes, others look to them as leaders. So, values, intention and courage are the things I value most in my clients. With those characteristics present, I am willing to go out of my way, to go above and beyond with them, offering my discretionary energy to them, in order to help them succeed.

Linda

MY BEST CLIENTS

When we decided to write this chapter, it was easy for me to select my best customers! Three very different organizations came to mind immediately. One is a salvaged auto parts company that merged with an electronic car parts ordering company; one is Kenton County Airport Board, the people responsible for the smooth and safe operation of the Greater Cincinnati International Airport; and another is Greater Cincinnati Water Works, a major utility in the Cincinnati area.

Even though these organizations differ widely in what they do, they're very similar in terms of their organizational culture and leadership approach. That's why I love them like I do.

Kenton County Airport Board (KCAB for short) has been a client for a dozen years, while Car-Part.com has only been a client for four years. One relationship evolved out of a professional association membership and the other was a referral from a colleague in the HR field. You never know where your next favorite client will come from! Let me share with you how these relationships began and grew to the point where they make my "short list" of favorite clients today.

I've been a member of my local professional association chapter since 1983 (which is amazing, since I'm only 27!). In the late eighties, I attended meetings on a regular basis because I was the chapter president and later, district and state director. I was enjoying the networking portion of a meeting one evening when I literally bumped into Rita Wetterstroem, the HR and Training Director for Kenton County Airport Board. She was gracious in accepting my apology for running into her shoulder, and we began a conversation about what we liked about the HR field, as well as its trials and tribulations. Afterward, we gravitated towards each other at meetings because we just clicked and enjoyed each other's company. She was very encouraging to me when I started my doctoral program and shared my intention of moving into the consulting field. "As a matter of fact," Rita said, "I'd like to be one of your first clients. I'll call you as soon as I have a project I need a consultant's help with." Well, that was nice, I thought. I figured that she might call me one day, but I wouldn't count on it. She called me.

In the consulting field, there are many types of clients. There are those who want a "rubber stamp" for their own ideas. There are those who are in over their heads and desperately need a consultant to do their job for them. There are those who have a firm grasp of their own skills and talents, yet know when to call on another's expertise to shore up their own competencies. Rita is in the latter category. I picked up the phone one morning and heard her cheerful voice saying, "It's time for me to become more strategic. I'd like to do strategic planning for my division and lead by example for the other divisions here. Will you help me?" Of course, I said I would. I led the strategic planning process for my division when I worked for the Sixth Circuit Court of Appeals, and had worked with a couple other clients already as a consultant. I had an approach that had proven to be successful that I wanted to share with Rita and her four-person team. She and her team have been apt pupils, absorbing ideas and best practices with a hearty appetite. Instead of always saying, "We can't," they're more likely to say, "Why not?"

Some clients are very formal and businesslike and some are casual in their approach and personality. Rita is more laid back. Her department "feels" friendly when you walk in the door. People remember your name and greet you with questions about your family and latest activities. When it's time to get to work, Rita stays focused and we always have results at the end of our time together. However, if in the middle of the "work" part a team member needs some personal encouragement, she takes the time out to provide it. Rita reads my books and articles, gives me feedback, and asks me questions. She's a deep thinker who may take a while to give that feedback . . . but when she's ready, her comments are well worth listening to.

Rita and I worked together for fourteen years, until her retirement last year. Now her successor still calls on me when she has an appropriate project that fits my talents (or those of someone on my team). And yes, I still stay in contact with Rita for the occasional lunch!

Rita also referred the other six directors within KCAB to me when they expressed an HR-related need or concern, and they still call on me from time to time. If I'm not the best fit for a project, I let them know and refer them to another capable consultant. My focus is on getting the organization the assistance they need, not on grabbing more business. My collaboration with this client has been fruitful and challenging, and it's one I treasure.

Let me turn to another great client, Car-Part.com, and tell you about my first meeting with their CEO, Jeff Schroder. He came into the room wearing cut-off blue jeans and a tee-shirt, with a bottle of water in his hand. His hair was slightly disheveled and it was clear he was still mentally wrestling with another issue from a previous meeting. He looked like he was—maybe—thirty.

Looks can definitely be deceiving! Jeff is closer to forty than thirty; he can easily multitask and mentally juggle two or three issues at a time. Jeff can afford to buy tailored suits and wing-tip shoes of the highest quality; he just chooses not to. He is brutally honest with himself and others. Early on during our first meeting Jeff said to me, "You don't have to be nice to me. I can take the truth." Well, I am always tactful and nice . . . and I always tell him the truth.

Car-Part.com is a sister company to an auto-salvage yard in Northern Kentucky. When I first pulled into the drive for my first meeting, I thought I was in the wrong place! To my left and right were cars of all types with missing tires, windshields, and seats. In front of me was a small stucco building that smelled of 10W-40 motor oil when I walked in the door. A young man with grease up to his elbows stood at the counter and I explained that I was looking for Car-Part.com and must have the wrong address. "No ma'am," he smiled, "you just have to walk over to that warehouse across the gravel parking lot." As I walked across the gravel and up a wooden staircase to Jeff's office, it occurred to me that high heels and a business suit probably weren't the right choice of wardrobe for this meeting . . . but, it actually turned out just fine.

Over the past few years, I've helped Jeff and his team with such projects as strategic planning, hiring a vice president of Human Resources, and coordinating CEO Roundtables. The first project I worked on with Jeff was helping him design an all-employee meeting, which was coming up in about three weeks. He had been referred to me as a potential speaker for one session of the two-day meeting. When I sat down with him and his staff, I asked, "What's the theme of your meeting, and what do you have planned so far, so I know how to tie in my portion with everything else?" They all just looked at one another and laughed. Jeff said, "We don't exactly have very much planned yet . . . so if you have any ideas, that would be really helpful." I did, and we ended up working some long days to prepare for what turned out to be an excellent employee event. Jeff was nice enough to invite my husband and me to join them in a dinner cruise the first evening of the meeting, which helped me bond with the employees even more. My dedication to his success earned Jeff's respect, and I've been happily doing projects with him and his company since.

In a small company, a few people have a broad scope of responsibilities, and so, as their management consultant, I similarly have a broad scope of responsibilities. This means that occasionally I have to move out of my comfort level and learn some new tricks myself, which I'm happy to do for Car-Part because I enjoy working with the staff so much. Recently, I found myself pouring over the Americans with Disabilities Act and related court cases to determine whether Car-Part needed a public restroom in specific sections of an expansion project they're planning. That little reading excursion convinced me to step up my efforts to help them find an HR person!

Car-Part.com is quite simply a team of plain spoken, hardworking, talented people who search for people like me who want to help them grow. There are only a few clients who have my cell phone *and* home number. Car-Part does, because I don't want to miss out on any of the action—I wouldn't miss it for the world!

Just last year, I began working for Greater Cincinnati Water Works, a utility company in the Greater Cincinnati area, helping them develop a diversity initiative and to train 600 managers and employees on ways to leverage different skills, talents, and perspectives. This is another favorite client because of the people in the organization. This group of people has reminded me that my work is my calling, not just a way to earn a living. When I've been in training sessions, individuals have asked sincere questions about their role in helping their workplace stay harassment free. They've made terrific suggestions about how their coworkers and they can be more inclusive and break down stereotypes. I've learned from the people in this organization, and I've been affirmed in my role as their consultant as well.

Recently, I finished a pilot program in preparation for rolling out company-wide training over the course of the next four months. One of the training committee team members, a line supervisor, has been very supportive during all our planning meetings and trial runs. He's tough, though . . . he doesn't accept anything less than the best in terms of advice, ideas, and training. He attended the pilot program and, as usual, was in the front with a smile on his face and a willingness to participate and share his thoughts. I thought the training went well, but I was waiting for his feedback as I was picking up evaluations and preparing to leave for the day. He came up to me and said, "This was a fine workshop. You made some excellent points and really drew people in. This is obviously a mission for you, not just a job." I thanked him for his comments and his active participation along the way, and told him how much that meant to me. He said, "Can I give you a hug?" Of course, I said yes. Then I asked him what I did to deserve that. His answer? "For being you and sharing yourself so unselfishly." I don't ever cry in front of clients . . . but I came darn close that day.

In order to have "best clients," it's necessary to be a "best consultant" in every sense of the word. If we're willing to actively listen, always provide our best effort, and have a strong sense of values that is evident our work, there will be clients like Rita, Jeff, and Michelle who want to partner with us—for the long haul.

Terri

LESSONS LEARNED

Of necessity, Linda and I wrote the earlier sections of this chapter separately, and then combined our thoughts to give you some "lessons learned."

We both found the results bordering on the bizarre. While Linda resides in Cincinnati, she chose to profile two Kentucky firms; I live in Northern Kentucky and chose to profile two Ohio firms. We discussed this for a while in our kitchen table conversations. How did this happen? Was this the unconscious competitiveness of two competitors, turned collaborators, trying to make some point? Was it an attempt to one-up the other author? What was it?

In the final analysis, we determined two things:

First, most consultants choose their first client as one of their top three all-time best clients. These are the clients that helped us get started, and it seems only natural.

Second, we concluded that our choice of "best clients" was an unconscious attempt to demonstrate our new collaborative efforts, not our competitiveness. Linda's focus has been on larger clients and she chose her smallest client; my focus has been on smaller clients and I chose my largest client. Our unconscious efforts were to find common ground, not competition.

There is a learning opportunity in every situation. Without a conversation and analysis, however, we would not have found the real reason for our choices. When you have spent as many years in the corporate environment as we both had, competitiveness would have been quite normal. We learned that our behavior, while tested in this exercise, was a direct reflection of our unconscious intent to build on the collaborative initiative we had begun. Writing this chapter could have pulled us apart; instead it brought us closer together.

11

Client Challenges and Difficulties

"It is common sense to take a method and try it. If it fails, admit it frankly and try another. But above all, try something."
—Franklin D. Roosevelt

Terri

CLIENT CHALLENGES AND DIFFICULTIES

Clients can be challenging and difficult. As consultants, we try to manage the expectations of clients and delight them, but it isn't always possible. Sometimes we don't listen well enough, sometimes our own egos get in the way, and sometimes neither the client nor the consultant is communicating at their best. Why? We are all human beings, and even the best consultants (and clients) do make mistakes. How well we deal with those mistakes, addressing the issue, confronting ourselves, and remedying the situation as best we can is what separates the women from the girls.

CHALLENGES—SCOPE CREEP

One of the most common challenges to business consultants is scope creep: the original boundaries of a project expand. For example, you have an outline of the project, the goals established, the schedule mapped out, and the price approved. Then, the client asks you to do one more thing. He thinks it is included in the scope of work; but you don't. When these add-ons are small—i.e. take an extra hour or two, I just do the additional work, often without even mentioning that I think this is beyond the project's scope. When I anticipate that these add-ons will take a more significant time investment to complete, I renegotiate the contract. Here's what I recommend when calculating that additional investment: first, ask yourself how easy the client is to work with; next, assess the potential for future work with the client beyond this project; and lastly, determine whether you like working with the person involved. Then, I decide how to proceed with the additional work, and how to discuss it with my client. There is a cost to everything we do; when we say yes to something, we say no to something else.

CHALLENGES—TIME CREEP

Time creep occurs as frequently as scope creep. The client is in a hurry, but in the middle of the project, there's another fire to put out. That means the project is going to take more time—and that's the same time that you had planned to work on another project, for another client. When you are in a small consulting practice that can mean scrambling to manage more clients and more projects than possible at one time. This also means that you're going to have to take more of your time to reschedule meetings, with a resulting increase in emails, phone calls, etc. To accommodate this, I have learned to build in a flat communication fee per month. Therefore, when the scope remains the same, but the time extends, you can at least recover the extra time to accommodate the rescheduling function. After fifteen years in the business, I have begun adding two hours per month for these communication fees, for each month of the contract.

Of course, when I am successful in value-based pricing, this will no longer be necessary. However, in the meantime, adding a communication fee does two things. First, it eliminates documentation for the phone calls and emails (a time saving to me) and secondly, allows me to recapture some of the money that may otherwise be lost.

There's another time loss that I have not found a way to recapture and that is attention time. Attention time is how I describe the smooth flow of continuing with a project from start to finish where a good memory keeps you on track as much as the project schedule. Project information remains top of mind and allows you to maintain that flow from project start to finish, even when you are juggling multiple projects. A delay means that you move on to the next project and your memory of the last step of the initial project begins to fade, until you have to refresh your memory by reviewing the documents before you proceed. I have not found an effective way to recover these lack-of-momentum costs.

CREATING OPPORTUNITIES FROM CHALLENGES

Firing Clients

While I have never fired a client in the middle of a project, I have nevertheless fired a client after the first project and refused to do business with them again. There's some money I don't need.

Sometimes, you simply walk away once the project is completed.

You have a reputation to protect and you have to determine the best way to do that. My reputation is all that I have that precedes me into any situation; I don't want it tarnished.

Linda

I've only had to fire one client in all my years of consulting, and it wasn't a difficult choice, really. I had just finished defending my dissertation in early 1995. Four years of consulting and being a full-time doctoral student had taken a huge toll on me mentally and physically. I was, well . . . cranky.

In the fall of 1994 I had agreed to work with a nonprofit agency to do some work on writing job descriptions and performance reviews. For someone with a background in HR, this wasn't a difficult task—just time consuming. The person who invited me in to work with her was a delightful person and I enjoyed the process. As I was finishing the project, a new person was brought in as her boss, a fellow who was not so delightful.

In fact, the new boss was loud, arrogant, and seemed to relish opportunities to put down his staff in front of others, myself included. He was abrupt and harsh when he asked questions or provided direction. I thought he didn't like me, but, evidently, he thought I was all right because when I finished the initial project he asked me to submit a proposal to work on the next project phase. He would be the liaison for this project, not the "delightful" woman I worked with before. That gave me pause. However, I wasn't exactly swimming with clients at that point so I agreed to submit a proposal.

The client demanded changes in the proposal three times. For pricing? No. For additional components of the work? No. He wanted changes in the wording of the proposal, such as revising phrases like "Deliverables for Phase One" to "Outcomes for Phase One." He called me at eight o'clock on a Saturday evening for the last round of changes, and he wanted it "on my desk" by 10:00 a.m. on Sunday. I was going out to a much-needed "alone-time" dinner with my husband that night, and I had planned to go to church the next morning. I made a split-second decision during that telephone conversation, and told my client that I wasn't the person for the project. I suggested that he pursue other proposals and announced that I would not be submitting one after all. As I went out that evening, I felt a hundred pounds lighter. (I later heard that a colleague took the project and fired the client after Phase One!)

HANDLING DIFFICULT SITUATIONS

Clients are not right 100 percent of the time, as the examples above indicate. We are not right 100 percent of the time, either. However, the client is right 99 percent of the time. Difficult situations are simply that—difficult. Usually, they are not impossible.

Most of the time, there are only simple misunderstandings, and those can be handled with a "sit-down" meeting with the client. We all make assumptions, we all have a certain set of expectations, and sometimes we don't make all of those clear up front. We learn and we go on. Most of the time, there is a positive outcome and we learn from one another. I think that is healthy. I don't shy away from confrontational meetings, nor do I like them. Most of the time, a confrontational meeting is unnecessary, but a conflict resolution meeting may be. Conflict is good, but negative conflict is not. Healthy discussions of both sides of the coin help all of us achieve what we really need, and most of the time what we want. In the difficult times, I remember Mick Jaeger's song lyrics: "You can't always get what you want, but if you try sometime, you get what you need."

Handling conflict with a client is the same as handling conflict with anyone else. There are a few tenets that I follow:

- **Choose the right time**—Address the problem as soon as

possible, but not too soon. If emotions are running high, then choose a time after a break to allow everyone to cool down. If you wait too long then memories fade and time alters the impact of immediate action.

- **Choose the right place**—a private location where a person can feel that he or she can say what needs to be said, without others overhearing the conversation.
- **Choose the right battle**—remember that your goal is to find a solution to the problem, not to "win," not to blame, and not to change the individual. Not all battles are worth fighting.
- The objective is to satisfy the client and to keep this or anything similar from occurring again.
- **Choose the right person**—the individuals on both sides of the conflict should be the individuals who can resolve the problem.
- **Choose the right words**—emotion-laden words will not help solve the problem, blaming will not solve the problem. Describe the problem and the impact of the behavior as you see it and/or listen as your client does the same. Be direct, specific and constructive in any description of the problem.
- **Choose to care**—if the individual knows that you care, your comments are more likely to be heard. If no one is listening or only one party is listening, then the conflict is likely to go unresolved.

Many times there is nothing you can do to "go back" and change what happened. In that case, you can only plan appropriately for future events. In this case, I try to ask the same questions that the U.S. Army asks:

"What happened?"

"Why did it happen?"

"What can we do to keep it from happening again?"

I have found this approach to work in most situations where conflict has occurred. Without trust and respect we have no communication. Therefore, reestablishing trust and demonstrating respect for the individual will enable you to resolve the issue and save the relationship. This is the ultimate goal.[ix]

WHEN YOU ARE READY TO QUIT CONSULTING

Terri

Consulting is not easy work. Many people aren't cut out for it. But for those of us who love what we do—as Linda and I do—we can't even imagine doing anything else. There are, however, times when you are ready to quit. There is not enough work or there is too much work. There is not enough money . . . or there is too . . . no, there's never been too much money, come to think of it. We both deserve the money we receive because we both earn it. Our client organizations are better off for having hired us to do this work; most times, the benefits are far in excess of what they paid us.

Healthy skepticism, even about your own profession, is good. We all need time to reevaluate. Before working for myself, I didn't stay longer than seven years with any employer. In retrospect, I went into those employment situations just as I do with a consulting client or project. I had specific goals to accomplish and I accomplished them. Then, I moved on. The only thing different in the consulting world is that many of my clients have been with me for longer than seven years; some more than double that. With some, I have a lifetime relationship, regardless of whether or not we do business with one another again.

I have known some clients since 1995. If they graduate to hiring a full-time high-level HR person because they had grown to that point, I feel as proud as a parent. I stay in touch. In fact, I actually have done that, as described in an earlier chapter, with one client who graduated.

ix Definitions differ for the terms goal and objective. My definition of goal is the ultimate priority; and objective is a sub-set of a goal.

We later worked together as partners on a three-year project.

In the end, it's those relationships that keep me consulting. I think, "How could I leave them?" I love the flexibility of my consulting work and I have never minded working long hours—it is just part of what makes me, me. Hard mental work to me is as healthy as physical exercise. When I think I have seen everything—something new pops up. When I think I have all the answers, I visit a classroom, and I always get one question that makes me think harder and longer than I have before.

≈

Linda

My longest "real job," for the Sixth Circuit Court of Appeals, lasted six years. Six loooooong years. The people I worked with were wonderful. The work was too predictable, too routine. Consulting is not predictable; it's not routine! Some of my clients have been with me for ten or more years. I agree with Terri that consultant-client relationships can be long lasting and meaningful. When I walk into many of my clients' offices, I feel like I am a part of their day-to-day work world.

I know when I feel I'm part of a client's team. Small things happen, really, that add up to that feeling of belonging. Recently, I was given a security badge at one company so I could walk unescorted to various conference rooms where meetings I would be attending were going to be held. I didn't have to be escorted, like a "visitor." In fact, occasionally new employees come up to me and ask for directions! (It's a maze-like, huge office building.) I guess I walk around like I work there . . . and I do.

The COO of another client company called me recently and asked if I would mind having coffee or lunch with a prospective vice president. The candidate was not only likely for the VP position—he was considered a high potential person for the COO's position one day. I was honored that the COO thought enough of my judgment to ask this of me. Of course, I said yes!

≈

SUMMARY

One of the most interesting aspects of consulting for us has been the opportunity to work with a variety of people with widely different perspectives and outlooks. This diversity of clients can be a challenge, yet it's what makes the work so interesting. We look at consulting as an opportunity to learn and grow ourselves—and the assurance that there will never be a dull moment!

12

How We Built Relationships With Subcontractors and Employees

erri

Sometimes it seems as though those of us in the HR field have done a 180-degree turn the past thirty years in our attitudes toward employees.

When you asked people thirty years ago why they chose HR as a profession, you were likely to hear one of two responses, or both. First, "I like people" or second, "I just fell into it".

Today, it seems as though the individuals who choose HR don't "just fall into it," they are students of HR through the classroom and extended study. And, they don't seem to like people.

Thirty years ago, and sometimes today, HR professionals are not respected. Individuals who choose this profession seem to have a difficult time getting "a seat at the table." Maybe it's for the opposite reason that it was thirty years ago: perhaps you have to have a business approach and a human approach at the same time. I think so.

You need to *like* people and *believe in* people to be successful in fields like Human Resource Management, but you must pair that with the ability to handle not being liked by everyone. You also have to know and understand the business in which you are operating. The subject of learning the business cannot be overstated—learn, not only about the financials, but also about the actual operations.

In my first professional position as a marketing manager, then a human resource manager with a city bus operation, I was fortunate that Edward A. Harvey was my general manager. Under his guidance, I spent time in each department, including two weeks in the maintenance department (I loved the brake lathes!), numerous weeks in the scheduling department, and I learned how to drive a bus, all as part of learning the business. Most of the managers objected: they did not want a "girl" around their business. (While I did not recognize it at the time, supporting me had a cost to it, and Ed Harvey paid that price on my behalf.) I will be forever grateful to him for that. Eventually, when the managers learned that I could provide them with better candidates for their open positions because of that training, they reluctantly said it was OK for others to do what I had done.

Later in my career, I was fortunate to have a Ph.D. food scientist, Jim Steinke, who was as curious about human resources as I was about the science of the flavor business. He agreed to teach me the business from his perspective. The manufacturing of flavors was the easy part of the business to understand and one that I learned quickly. The science was an entirely different matter. Hour upon hour we spent teaching one another about our respective fields, reading recommended books and asking questions of one another. Industry mentors can be invaluable to your learning. And, as with Ed, I was grateful for the investment Jim made in my career.

In the case of consulting, the business owner can help you, but you will find that you must do a great deal of research on your own. If you are eager to learn the business, are a fast learner, and have prior experience in that field or a similar one, so that you can hold onto the new concepts you learn, and most people will help in your operations education. This, for me, is one of the most fascinating aspects of consulting. I am constantly learning about new businesses, new industries, new domains, and can then cross-pollinate the business with concepts from one industry to another. This applies equally well to working with small businesses and nonprofit organizations. Each type of organization can learn something from the other, and I have the opportunity to share concepts that are relevant from one type to another.

We build relationships in many ways—all of which require choices. The first choices are those you make for yourself—in response to what you want or need. You choose a profession, an industry and one or more organizations. You choose your friends –the people you share your most intimate thoughts with—the people who know you best. You choose your colleagues—the people you choose to work with—this often includes people you choose as sub-contractors. You choose your associates, frequently including employees and people in the community with whom you work or serve. Lastly, you choose your acquaintances—lots of acquaintances—the people whose names you know—and who know your name.

Importantly, the closer the individuals are to you, the more important that it is you share their values. Acquaintances do not have to share your values, but your friends do. You view the values of your closest peers through the lens of their behavior. And, for everyone else, you need to have a healthy dose of both skepticism and respect for what they bring to the table. Don't ever underestimate the value or potential harm of any individual—associate, colleague, or acquaintance—can bring to you individually or to your organization. And, that goes for the relationships you have with receptionists, plumbers, and CEO's, as well.

Terri

COMPLEMENTING ONE ANOTHER'S EDUCATION AND EXPERIENCE

Unlike Linda, I do not have a doctoral degree; therefore, I frequently employ sub-contractors who do. Many of these individuals are teaching professors at one of our local universities, and we're fortunate to have three major institutions of higher learning within just thirty miles.

Beyond their educational credentials, I look for subcontractors who have real-world working experience, as well as the latest information and theory within their area of expertise.

On the other hand, I use a technology expert who doesn't have a college degree. Instead, he has thirty years of experience in technology and is the author of twenty-seven books, not counting the translation editions, on the subject of technology.

My seven goals for employing subcontractors are as follows:

1. Real world work experience—a professor who has never worked in industry does not meet that standard;
2. An expert—possessing leading-edge knowledge within their field of expertise;
3. A minimum of fifteen years and preferably more within the field of their expertise;
4. The ability to interact well with my clients;
5. Prior experience with the individual in a different work environment or on a different consulting project;
6. Outstanding communication skills; and
7. A well-rounded individual, with varied interests.

I have not had any positive experiences with students as subcontractors. It seems to me that students have expectations today that are beyond the mere opportunity to learn and gain experience. My experience suggests they want to be treated as an experienced professional, with the attendant income expectations. When I find someone who exhibits the right attitude and desire, perhaps I will change my mind. Yes, a student has something to offer an employer, but the professor has more. Which one would you choose? My preference is to pay, relatively speaking, a professor $100 per hour rather than a student $50 per hour. I get a better return for my dollars and no expectations that I should spend my time in training them. You pay for education and training.

EMPLOYEES

During the first fifteen years of my business, I have had two outstanding operations managers and a couple of virtual assistants (off-site administrative assistants). Both the operations managers had more experience than was required for the job, and both were transitioning from one type of employment to another. Both had made more money before coming to me, and both left my company for more money and better benefits. But, the transition for them was an enormous help to my practice and, hopefully, some benefit to them too.

I would employ each of the operations managers again in a heartbeat, given the opportunity. I was more productive while they were with me. They took care of the back-of-the-office tasks, as well as represented my firm in the community. In both situations, I had significant personal issues to handle, as well as the obligations to complete work responsibilities for my clients. Both managers were valuable because they had the right skill mix at the right time for my business and for me, personally.

In the end, keeping them was unfair. They were both ready for other challenges and, thankfully, my personal dilemmas had been resolved. I won't ever forget their kindness during those difficult times, or the productive impact they had on my business. There is a time for everything;

and it was time for them to go, just as it had been time for them to come to me.

Two other individuals, on the other hand, did not work out as planned. They are both fine individuals and both had different sets of skills, but I underestimated the time necessary to devote to their learning and development. I am not saying that I wouldn't do that again, but my expectations would be different.

SUBCONTRACTORS VS. EMPLOYEES

In the past few years, the IRS has been cracking down on employers who have misclassified independent contractors. The theoretical base of these crackdowns is that independent contractors aren't receiving the benefits they deserve, such as unemployment insurance, worker's compensation insurance, or health insurance. A critical look at the proposal would suggest that the government sees an opportunity to generate more taxes by reclassifying these individuals from contractors to employees, ensuring that the government receives its share of the taxes. While seeking new sources of income for the federal government is a laudable thing to do, especially in the times of such massive federal debt, the government might reconsider their efforts in this regard. Before the end of this decade it is likely that only fifty percent of the available work force will be employed by others, as in the traditional "employee" definition. The remaining fifty percent will be unattached "non-employee" workers—temporary workers, freelancers, consultants, etc. However, that's a subject for another time.

This is an area of law to watch closely as you choose whether to employ subcontractors or employees.

da

During my first year of consulting, I was challenged to find enough work for myself, let alone having the financial ability to hire employees or subcontractors. About halfway through my second year, however, I found that clients or potential clients were asking for expertise I didn't have or needing time that I didn't have to give them because I was in graduate school. The logical choice was for me to bring on subcontractors because I felt I was too new as a business owner to risk hiring employees with the ongoing commitment of paying someone a regular wage.

Deciding to bring on subcontractors was the easy part; finding the right people was the hard part. Most of the time, I have made the right choices over the years, but, not always. I'll share in this chapter what I learned about working with employees and subcontractors, mostly from mistakes I made.

One of my first clients was a medical facility that had a small human resources staff that often needed supplementary HR expertise. One of my assignments involved developing and administering a multi-rater feedback instrument (a performance appraisal/career development system that requests feedback from supervisors, peers and employees who report directly to the individual) to several mid-level and frontline supervisors. Compiling the results took a fair amount of time but was manageable. Meeting with recipients of the feedback and coaching them to develop an action plan around the results was manageable. My time crunch occurred in the preparation of bar charts that summarized the numerical scores on the instrument. Not only was this time consuming, it was outside my Microsoft Excel and PowerPoint expertise. So, I decided to find a subcontractor to take care of this part of the project. I called a colleague and asked for suggestions. He provided me with a name and phone number of a three-person word processing company run by a female entrepreneur. I thought, "Great . . . I'll give the business to another woman trying to make a success of entrepreneurship." I dropped by her office and talked to her briefly before I left my first set of results for her to prepare. I should have talked to her longer and asked for examples of similar work—and references. I should have been nervous when she informed me that the project would take a week to complete and the fee seemed a bit pricey.

The bottom line to this story is that I continued to work with this subcontractor for three months. Often, she wouldn't have my job ready when I arrived at the agreed-upon pick-up date and time. Often, I had to make last-minute corrections to the work before I gave it to my client. Even though her work was late, her invoices weren't, and payment was demanded within seven days. My client usually didn't pay me sooner than three weeks after invoicing, so I wasn't coming out ahead on that deal. At the end of each month, I'd share my concerns with the business owner and she'd promise her team would do better. After fixing their mistakes one time too many, I advised the owner that we'd no longer be working together. The unsatisfactory relationship wasn't exclusively her fault—it was mine as well. I learned from that experience.

If you decide first what your core values are, what your mission statement is, and your vision for how you want to position yourself and your company in the marketplace, you have a foundation for setting expectations for subcontractors and employees. I encourage you to interview each prospective subcontractor as thoroughly as you do potential employees. Talk with references, previous employers, and other consultants for whom they've worked.

I recommend that you have, and faithfully use, a written subcontractor agreement so terms and expectations from both sides are clear. An example of an agreement that I have used over the years is included in Appendix 6. This includes my company's operating philosophy, payment terms, and confidentiality issues. I typically add sections to this agreement tailored to a particular project around scope of the work and deadlines.

EMPLOYEES

I won't discuss specific employees that haven't worked out over the years (there have been two), however, I will share some thoughts about finding the best and the brightest and ensuring that the relationship gets off to a good start, and stays on track.

There's no doubt that most people work to make a living and deserve fair compensation for their contributions. I've made the mistake of hiring people who came into consulting only because of an (unrealistic) expectation that they could instantly become rich, not for the love of the field and contributions they could make. They tended to make decisions that weren't focused on the client, but rather on expanding billable hours. Now I hire people who want to make a good living, of course, but who have a passion for learning and sharing what they've learned. I discover this passion by asking the right questions during the interview process. Some of my favorite questions are:

Take me through a time when you took a project from idea stage to launch stage.

Describe the way you work under tight deadlines.

In a team environment, are you a motivator, a leader, or a cheerleader?

Tell me about a time when you persuaded someone to try a particular approach to solve a problem.

How do you determine top priorities when you're scheduling your time?

In the past three years, what part of your professional skill set have you improved the most?

How do you measure success?

Even with a solid interview and sound decision about who to bring on board, I've found there are times when my communication with subcontractors or employees has not been exactly crystal clear. The key was discovering that miscommunication before there was an adverse impact on clients. For instance, one of my subcontractors didn't understand that he was expected to coordinate meetings with one of his assigned clients through me. This was so that I could keep track of who was in which organization and when, to help me make assignments based on availability and expertise. I received a call one day from an out-of-town client asking if I could please call them before my subcontractor "just dropped in" for meetings. Some of these meetings weren't in the proposal and hadn't been agreed to by myself or the client—so I couldn't invoice for those hours! My subcontractor was new to the consulting field, so at first he didn't understand that you don't drop in on clients the way one might walk down the hall in a corporation to chat with a coworker.

My subcontractors and employees have bolstered my expertise and made me look good over the years, and I'm so grateful for that. Recently, a potential client asked me to make a mini-presentation as a sample of how I developed and conducted management training. The selection team was impressed and I made the "short list" of consultants they were considering. I received a call from the client asking if my designated back-up for this type of training could also do a mini-presentation so they could be assured of the same quality. My subcontractor made herself available on very short notice, presented a small program segment, and totally impressed the selection team. They liked her so much that they expanded their budget so we could both be included in the project!

I'm currently working on another project that involves developing job descriptions for staff at a university. This is a huge undertaking that involves employee interviews and lots of analysis. I love interviewing people because I'm an off-the-chart extrovert (I'm not as fond of actually writing job descriptions and developing organization charts). My subcontractor loves this aspect of the project and is painstakingly precise. The client is extremely happy with the product, and I'm so grateful not to have to tax the other side of my brain unnecessarily.

Occasionally, my clients have so enjoyed working with a subcontractor or employee that they've offered him or her a position at their company! I take this as a compliment. Still, I need to protect the intellectual property that belongs to my company. I don't ask people to sign a non-compete agreement; however, I do have a section in my subcontractor agreement that prohibits people from taking concepts designed by my company to be used elsewhere without my consent. I am very proud when people take career skills they've acquired while working with my company and use them wisely to help organizations around the world. As Martha Stewart says, "It's a good thing."

Sometimes I have been asked to be a subcontractor for other consultants. This can be fun, since there is an opportunity to learn from others, and sometimes I get pulled into work on contracts that I cannot get on my own. As with anything, experience is a wonderful teacher. I have learned that there are some pitfalls in working as a subcontractor that can be avoided with attention and forethought.

The first couple of times I worked as a subcontractor, in my early consulting years, I didn't know what I didn't know about establishing contracts prior to starting a project, and small but significant details such as business cards.

I was doing a series of workshops as a subcontractor and during the training, a participant asked for my card so that she could follow up with some questions. I didn't have a card for the consultant company for which I was working; I just had my own business cards. Since I was there on behalf of another company, I didn't want to give my business cards, but I thought it would look unprofessional if I had nothing to offer. I compromised and gave her my company card with the number of the consultant I was working with as the direct contact line. As soon as possible, I arranged to have business cards with the other company where I was listed as an associate consultant.

Ensuring that consulting philosophies are in tune is a critical aspect of working as a subcontractor or hiring others as subcontractors. I have learned to request references for potential subcontractors just as if I was hiring an employee in corporate America. I ask questions like, "What are values that you hold that you wouldn't ever compromise, no matter what?" and, "Describe the analysis process you use to make decisions." I don't want subcontractors or lead consultants I work with to be clones or mini-me's, but I do want to work with people who have similar values and work ethic!

13

The Balancing Habit

"Life is like riding a bicycle. To keep your balance you must keep moving."
—Albert Einstein

rri

Half of the women who work for themselves rank loving freedom and flexibility as the number one reason they like working for themselves. Being more creative and having more fulfilling careers are reasons two and three. [48]

In our contemporary society where sleep outranks sex as the most desirable activity, no wonder that women want flexibility in their lives.

Sex is one of the four primary drivers in the oldest part of our brain—that part of our brain that controls our survival behavior. The other drivers are fight, flight and food. Without sleep our bodies will not function; with only a little sleep our bodies do not function "on all cylinders", meaning that we are vulnerable to predators. We will fight for sleep since not doing so threatens our very existence.

From regular discussions with our fellow consultants, we developed the following seven point checklist for success in life balance. You can rank each of the following on a scale of one to ten for your current success in achieving balance, then rank it again as you view the life of a consultant. You may even want to try it again once you have finished reading the book and decided to become a Woman Business Owner (WBO).

The WBO Balance and Success ScoreCard				
Rank 1-10	**Current**	**Consultant**	**WBO**	**Desired**
Freedom & Flexibility				
Creativity				
Fulfillment				
Reaping the rewards of hard work				
Being my own boss				
Family time				
Fun				

"Women want it all. We can have it all. We just can't have it all at the same time. Our time frame must be our own life calendar."
Terri Bonar-Stewart, September, 2011

≈

We outgrew the navy blue suits; we can alter time. As Einstein told us, light is the only constant; time and space are relative. When *our* light (our clarity, illumination, our connection with the divine) is our vision, all other constraints are just temporary distractions. When we try to fit our vision and our goals into the artificial constraints of "normal" time, we create stress (actually *distress*) that shortens our lives. However, we can create balance by shifting the time and space in which we operate. This is time-shifting and space-shifting, not shape-shifting.[x]

Time-shifting can take the form of changing our routine to include or exclude activities. The most common time-shifting occurs when television shows or audio is locally recorded for later watching or listening. Some devices allow even shorter versions than those originally played, by allowing the consumer to eliminate commercials by fast-forwarding through them. This can cut a one-hour show down to forty-two minutes of viewing time. If you watch two hours of television per day, this is a savings of over thirty minutes.

I use the term space-shifting[xi] to describe *where* you decide to do work or play, sometimes intermingling the two. Sometimes sharing space, but not focused time, with someone else, such as doing your "work" or school homework while your child or spouse does the same.

We can also use our creativity in creating "blending" opportunities in our lives. I believe that we should work to improve the lives of our families and of our clients, as well as endeavor to improve our profession, and the communities in which we live—in other words, to be proactive community citizens. When I was thirty-three, my father planted a hundred walnut tree saplings, knowing that he would never live to see them become fully grown trees. I am reminded of the quote by Canadian pioneer, Nelson Henderson, "The true meaning of life is to plant trees, under whose shade you do not expect to sit."

x Shape-shifting is pulling ourselves out of alignment by acting as though we were someone we are not. Just as with the Star Trek characters, this shape-shifting takes its toll by shortening our lives.

xi Space shifting is sometimes used as a substitute for the term place-shifting which is technically defined as remote viewing over broadband.

BLENDING

Blending is another technique for creating a balanced life. "Blending" is the process of including two or more activities we care about into one experience. Here are a few ideas for blending:

1. Combining community service with family activities.
2. Including other individuals in family activities.
3. Introducing clients to one another at events you sponsor.
4. Making guests "company" and company "guests."
5. Linking friends and ideas.

My sister, Darla, took her four small sons to the local soup kitchen for homeless people when she went to volunteer. They were just big enough to fill water glasses; as they grew older, they could fill coffee cups, then actually serve the food. In this location, the director of the facility refers to the people she serves as "guests" and treats them accordingly. A child learning to treat homeless people as "guests" is a life value lesson. Combining the activities of serving in the community with your children is just one way of blending. Children learn what they live and these children, now all young men, now have a habit of giving back to the community in which they live.

On the other hand, I remember as a child that it felt uncomfortable to have "company" because the adults would first offer food and drink to guests, then just sit around talking. When people were family or "like family," they helped to do the cooking or gardening while they were talking. The concepts of treating strangers like family and family and friends like guests stuck with me. This is an unexpected and welcome experience for all concerned.

My grandmother gave me an early example of community blending when she took me with her to a quilting bee[xii] when I was young. The gift being created was a community quilt, usually for someone at the church who had fallen on hard times, and was a present that was filled with love. The stories that were told over those "bees" were weaving the fabric and the herstory of that community and became a warm comforter for both those creating the gift as well as, literally, for someone in need. Before my grandmother's time, the scraps of fabric were precious; during the Civil War, even needles were rare, and the time that women had away from their families and chores was rare and limited to those quilting bees.

Later, as a consultant, I had a client (a nun) who didn't have a family of any kind, anywhere. I invited her to Thanksgiving dinner with my family. That was a rare experience, sharing Thanksgiving dinner with a Catholic nun, when I wasn't Catholic. But, because I knew her as a client and came to know her as a friend, the result was a feeling of comfort and not discomfort. Unfortunately, the order did not take too well to our friendship, but as you know, when you make your customer your friend and you lose a customer, you still have a friend. Friends are much more valuable than customers.

Somewhere in my travels to adulthood, I heard the message that a person's level of intelligence was determined by what they talk about, in this order:

1. Things,
2. Other people, then
3. Ideas.

I can no longer determine the source of that information and we all talk about each of those. But regardless of the source, it stuck so tightly

xii A quilting bee is a group of women who jointly build one quilt at a time.

that I try to limit my discussion of *things* in my life. For me things are either useful or serve as personal expressions of beauty. Whether useful or beautiful, things are for me and my immediate family to use and enjoy, not items to display to impress other people. I try to talk about other *people* only when the comments are positive. I try to focus my attention on *ideas*. I must admit that one of my favorite activities is to introduce ideas to new people, people to new people, and to broker concepts that can lead people to innovation. Brokering has become embedded into my DNA. This, for me, is blending.

From my vantage point, it is productive to make blending and building of the community a part of each of our lives. We build community when we share experiences.

BALANCE: FREEDOM AND FLEXIBILITY

The World Future Society reports a trend in the next twenty-five year forecast: "Workers will increasingly choose more time over more money . . . In the twenty-first century . . . workers will increasingly choose to trade higher salaries for more time with their families. Nearly one-third of workers recently polled said they would prefer more time off rather than more hours of paid employment."

Nearly 80 percent of corporate women would give up some amount of money for more freedom and flexibility: nearly 30 percent would give up 20 percent of their income for the opportunity. [49]

The U.S. Department of Labor funded the national workplace flexibility project and published the results and guidelines for implementation. The original target audience was women business owners. Two years later, the project's audience expanded to include all business owners—both men and women—in small to mid-sized companies.[50]

My small business clients who are primarily Lifestyle Entrepreneurs, report that a significant factor in why they run their own businesses is the opportunity to balance their personal lives.

History or Herstory

From the beginning of this democratic republic in which we live, "Republican Women" were charged with the morality of our country and the education of our children. The term "republican" is not a reference to a political party, but to the expansion of women's power in the new republic. The term coined in 1980 by author and historian Linda Kerber[51], describes the expansion of power sharing between men and women during the Revolutionary period in America. A woman's education became a vehicle by which mothers could pass on republican moral excellence to their children. As such, in the United States, females were first permitted to pursue an education because they were charged with teaching their sons and encouraging them to further their education.

Today, there is a strong correlation between the level of educational achievement of parents and the level of education achieved by their children, and the best indicator of a child's educational achievements is a mother's education.[52] As the conscience of society and the leader in educational pursuits, we believe that women hold a special place in society, regardless of our personal desires and aspirations to pursue a business of our own.

Mothers often feel that they have a choice between a personal life and a professional life – one or the other. Some decide it is an either or decision – they decide they can have both. This gender legacy places special opportunities and burdens on those of us who choose to pursue *it all.* Something has to give. We can choose to give up our lives, literally due to the stress of it all, or we can mold our desires into a timeframe that is unique to us.

I was thirty-four when my son was born; before that, I didn't believe I would have a family. If I hadn't had a child, I know I would have lived a happy and satisfying existence. I had no idea how having a child would so dramatically alter my life. And, there has never been one moment when I wished for things to be different. I was happy; he was a surprise, and the best surprise of my life. I thought I could manage to have it all, and I tried to have it all, all at once. That didn't work for me.

After starting my own business, I was much happier. I could run a business, raise a child, and participate in my community. I could not, however, initially garner the same level of money. In terms of income, I had gone from a high-powered, highly compensated, corporate job to a one-woman organization with no foreseeable income.

The choice I made was one where I could place my family first (at least when I needed to do so), and to fit a consulting practice around that. I reasoned that as the child-rearing years were over, I would have the opportunity to develop the business further. The challenge was to create something that would provide for my family financially, while "being there" for my family when we needed one another.

WHAT HAPPENS ON A BAD DAY?

Journal Notes
May 10, 2004

Working from home always brings unique challenges. On May 10, 2004, I returned from an early appointment and as always, checked my voice mail and email.

As I was checking the voice mail, something happened; perhaps the lines were crossed since I reached the 911 operator. I apologized that I must have dialed incorrectly.

I continued what I was doing and five minutes later, the doorbell rang. There are only so many cookie vendors who come to the door, since our community has a solicitation registration that discourages all but the Girl Scouts, and delivery services. I assumed that I was receiving another video to preview or office supplies that I had forgotten were to be delivered today. When the door bells rings, I hang up from checking messages and trek up the stairs to the front door. As I peek through the peephole, I see a police officer standing there. Of course, my first thought was of my twenty-one-year-old-son and his safety. But, I knew he was in the military, and if this were about him, the person at the door would have dressed in another type of uniform. I opened the door and he said, "I have a 911 call from this address."

I began to explain that I must have dialed the wrong number, and then I stopped myself and got to the bottom line— I said: "I'm OK. Everything is OK". He said that the call had been disconnected and that normally the dispatcher would have asked for my name and the problem, but I hung up, so they thought they would check.

I thanked him and told him again that everything was fine—that I appreciated him checking things out. He said "No problem" and "I was in the neighborhood." He was very gracious.

Two minutes later the phone rang, and I was back to work with a client. It was 10 p.m. before I even remembered to tell my husband that the police had come by today.

WHAT I DO TO MANAGE STRESS

A police officer appearing at the door, business calls being interrupted, personal text messages popping up—I feel stressed from all of these.

In order to create balance in my life, as it is with the constant up and down of business—too much one month, not enough the next, I use several techniques beyond just breathing deeply and drinking water.

While my exercise regime primarily involves walking and gardening, I use several other techniques for dealing with stress as well:

1. When it's raining, I watch old movies.
2. I take a long shower or hot bath.
3. I play in the dirt.
4. I practice Qigong, a martial art.
5. I read a funny book or watch a funny movie.

I began gardening when I was two, and I still love playing in the dirt. In 2007, researchers discovered that there is a scientific reason that playing in the dirt causes pleasure. Apparently there is a naturally occurring bacterium in dirt, *Mycobacterium vaccae* that was already known to help stimulate the immune system. This bacterium has been used in clinical in trials to treat patients with cancer. However, doctors were surprised when patients reported that since starting *M. vaccae* treatment their quality of life improved. Subsequent research revealed that the bacterium had activated neurons that produce serotonin, an effect that is also seen following treatment with antidepressant drugs.

M. vaccae is reportedly one of about ninety species of environmental mycobacteria (bacteria that exist in our environment and do not require a host to survive) and they are abundant in water as well as in dirt. Apparently, there is science behind our instinctive notions of taking soaking baths and playing in the dirt. I just know I feel better.

Old movies, especially those in the 1940s, were created to either reflect our presence in World War II or to create an escape to keep from thinking about the war. The latter-type of movies are my favorites. They are filled with optimism, they're morality plays of the time, and provide a sufficient story line to refocus my mind away from the day-to-day. Rainy day movies are comforting and inspiring. Movies that make you laugh are even more valuable.

This year, I have added massages and Qigong to my list of relaxation and stress-reduction techniques. These are both my exercise and my personal indulgence.

THE CHALLENGE OF BALANCE – THE TIARA AND THE TEDDY BEAR

Conducting training seminars on balancing your life and your stress is one of the offerings of my practice; these balance seminars are among the most challenging I present.

The first time I conducted a stress seminar was for the U.S. Postal Service. One might think that given the development of the term "going postal", I had addressed the most difficult audience that I would face. However, that was not the case.

The second time I presented this topic is *the one* I'll never forget. On September 12, 2001, I was scheduled to present "Effectiveness: Balancing Your Life and Your Stress" to the Kentucky Municipal Clerks Association Master Academy in Owensboro, Kentucky. I drove six hours to the conference on September 11, 2001, and heard on the radio the disaster we know as 9/11. Terrorism had come to our national shores; my intended presentation went out the door.

We lost one-third of the audience that night, with people returning to their respective Kentucky cities to assess what needed to be done right away. The rest remained, realizing that there would be mostly chaos the next day, waiting for more information on what had happened to our country and their cities and towns.

Talk about a stressed audience! We were a group out of balance, in a country out of balance. Resuming our balance would take time for all of us, but I had to get my own balance back before morning.

There is a saying in consulting—"Just trust the process." As I fell asleep from the fatigue of driving hour after hour as well as the shock, sadness and confusion we all felt on September 11, 2001, my brain continued working through the night. I trust my brain to work efficiently and effectively 24/7, which it does when I take care of it. When I awoke, I knew what I had to do.

I was talking to a group of non-traditional care-givers, for the most part. These were the women (and one man) who cared for the cities and citizens throughout Kentucky—the individuals who act behind the scenes and make our cities run smoothly, effectively and efficiently. These individuals were not prone to panic. I also knew from prior presentations to a smaller group of this constituency that they weren't accustomed to talking about their feelings.

I changed the presentation to first talking about what we knew at the time, then talking about the stress we were feeling. I indicated that before the morning was out we would talk about the tips and techniques for dealing with our own feelings and the feelings of others. I had set up the room, although it was 8 a.m., with the lights dimmed, the candles burning, and the soft music of *The Celestine Prophecy* playing in the background. While I know this is going to sound strange, I am going to share this anyway: when I do presentations on stress and balance, I carry with me a Teddy Bear and a Tiara. That morning, I used them to provide comfort and balance.

We helped each other through that horrible day. Since we tend to help one another in times of crisis, this day was no different. In fact, our need for group survival was heightened—that is the basis of what it means to be human. Because my role that day was to lead people toward healing—to listen, comfort and provide some techniques that could help them get through the next hours and weeks - and to prepare them to do the same for others once they returned home. That is what it means to be a consultant—to improve the situation.

I just turned down the opportunity to do a paid presentation in Chicago. I love Chicago, normally, and the topic requested is on generational differences which is the subject of one of my books. Yet, I said "no thanks" after learning that the conference is the last day of January. After paying for airfare or mileage, the planning committee could afford $400 as a fee. I didn't turn down the engagement because the fee is low . . . I turned it down because I don't want to travel to Chicago from Cincinnati in the dead of winter. It's an option I have because I can be flexible as a business owner—and I exercised the option! In my days in corporate America, I dragged myself through wind, snow, sleet and typhoons (literally) to get to work, on time, with a smile on my face. It's so wonderful to have the flexibility to stay snug and warm, if that's what I'd prefer.

Earlier in the chapter, Terri quoted Launch's research about women's willingness to give up 20 percent of their income in return for freedom and flexibility. I'm one who did just that. In 1991, I was the administrator (with a high salary) for a federal court, a complete benefit package, and an office "to die for." I admit that giving up the office was the most difficult part of leaving to start my own consulting practice. The office, in a court house dating back to the mid-1800s, was twenty-by twenty-six-feet, with a wall of floor to ceiling windows, walnut moldings, and antique furniture. You could land a helicopter on the big oak desk I had. My husband used to love to come and take me for lunch, just so he could hang out in my office. My office today is a converted bedroom in my home, and even though it's only a twelve-by-fourteen-foot space, it's all mine and overlooks our back yard and pool! The color scheme, country blue and white, with rose accents, makes me smile whenever I walk into the room.

Even though most days I'm sitting at my computer desk at 6:00 a.m., frequently I can take a few hours off like I did earlier this week to browse through antique shops with a friend. My work day typically runs from 6:00 a.m. until 4:00 p.m., five days a week, unless I have a dinner meeting, and then it runs longer. Most of the time, I have my evenings free to watch TV with hubby or play with my grandchildren. I do, however, need to be prepared to drop personal and family activities at a moment's notice and take care of a pressing business need. The day I'm writing this chapter is a perfect example of that situation. I received a call at 9:17 a.m. from an NBC reporter doing a story on older workers with younger bosses. He called me because I'm co-author of a book, titled *Bridging the Generations Gap*, which he had just read. He asked if he could have a news crew at my home office this afternoon at 1:00. I flew through the house, furiously clearing out dust bunnies, and straightening pillows! With my thirty minutes to spare, I'm writing on another chapter (because that keeps me calm). Such is my life.

Sometimes I have to be in my home office at odd hours because I have international clients. Recently, I took a power nap and woke up at 2:00 a.m. to get on a video conference with a client in Tokyo. I did my hair and makeup and was wearing a nice shirt and blazer. Since the IBM PC camera I have is focused on the shoulders up, I kept on my purple striped pj's and pink fuzzy slippers. The call came in and I became engrossed in the conversation. One of the callers asked for some information that I had in a file in my credenza . . . across the office from my computer desk. Without thinking, I got up and started across the room to get the file I needed. I was halfway across the room when it dawned on me that I was wearing my pj's! I was *so* busted. So, I got the file, came back to my desk, and went on with the conversation without so much as a comment. As soon we broke the connection, I sat and laughed for five minutes straight!

Terri watches old movies, takes long showers, and gardens to relax. I, too, have outlets that help me manage a stressful lifestyle. Once a month, I take myself to my day spa and get a luxurious pedicure and foot massage. When I leave, my breathing is slower and my frame of mind is calmer... and I have pretty feet. I highly recommend regular pedicures, manicures, or massages for this reason. If you've never tried yoga or t'ai chi, these are great activities as well. I've studied martial arts for many years and picked up t'ai chi along the way as a mental release and form of exercise. It's amazing what just thirty minutes a day can do for a body and soul!

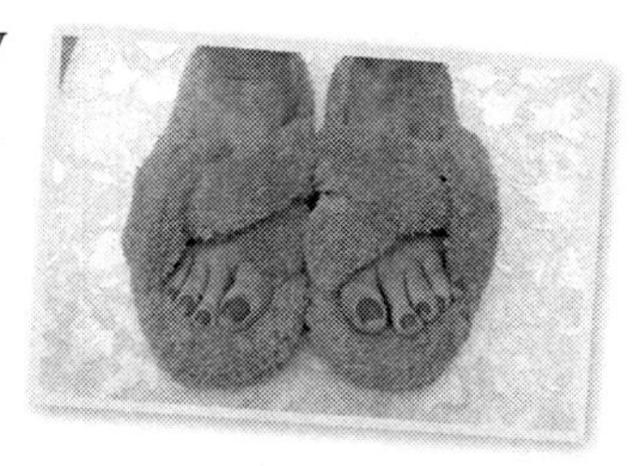

I guess I should insert a caveat here that *where* one chooses to do t'ai chi or yoga makes a difference. Right after my husband and I moved in to our home, I started going to our back deck to do my morning T'ai Chi ritual. Have you ever had the feeling someone was watching you? One morning as I was practicing a particularly strange looking movement, literally translated as holding the back end of a donkey, I felt that I was being watched. I glanced up and towards the house next door, and sure enough, the neighbors were on their deck with a cup of coffee in hand staring at me as though I had dropped in from another planet. I waved and kept right on going. They still look askance at me whenever we pass each other walking our respective dogs.

Terri captures ideas and thoughts in a journal. My reflection time occurs while I'm doing t'ai chi kadas. It's amazing what goes through my mind sometimes as I'm perched in some strange pose on my deck!

Yesterday afternoon was warm so I took myself outside to get some fresh air while I got my exercise. The fresh air made me think of airing differences of opinion . . . which made me think that I disagree with an interview approach a co-author of another book I'm writing wants to use for CEOs we're going to interview next month . . . which made me realize I was starting to get stressed because I don't believe his approach will be effective. So while I was "holding the back end of a donkey," I reflected on straightforward, yet respectful ways, I could share my concerns with my colleague. We met for coffee this morning and compromised in a way that's satisfactory to us both. I could have let this worry eat away at me and stress me out . . . but life is way too short.

From time to time, I'm asked to facilitate stress management workshops, either for a specific client or for Xavier University for public offerings. I just completed a one-day workshop recently, and that experience forced me to reflect on how well I'm managing my time and reducing stress. (I hate to just "tell" people something I'm not doing, or haven't at least tried, myself!) My key message in the workshops is this: You can't really manage time . . . it'll pass by whether you want it to or not. You can manage how well you use the time you have, with the choices you make.

This entire book is about choices, really. Terri and I chose to spend our time working for our own companies rather than in corporate America. We choose to work on weekends sometimes so we can take a weekday off. Now and then, I experience positive stress . . . the positive stress that comes from wanting to do my very best work for companies I love working with.

Whenever colleagues come to my home to work on a project, we work outside on my deck when the weather permits. I can easily take my laptop and cell phone outside with me since there's no reason to stay cooped up inside on a pretty day! My colleagues appreciate the opportunity to get some fresh air and take a dip in the pool to re-energize. Little things aren't just important—they're everything.

Of course, working outside isn't always as great as it sounds. On one warm and sunny September day, I invited a consultant I hadn't worked with before to have our first project planning meeting at my home. Since the weather was so pretty, I fixed a nice lunch and served it outside on our deck. Unfortunately, the bees decided it would be a good time for a meeting too . . . they began dive bombing almost immediately after we sat down! I was thinking "this is a great first impression" as we were grabbing dishes and running inside!

It is also harder, I've found, to get people to actually leave meetings at my house as opposed to when I was in a downtown office. I typically let visitors know that I'm available from time A to time B, and that usually works. Years ago, I met with a consultant I hadn't worked with previously and, since it was winter, we were meeting in my kitchen so I could fix hot chocolate when we needed sustenance. At the appointed end time for our meeting, I closed up my laptop and started pulling my notes into a pile. My colleague kept talking and made no move towards "closing up shop." I thanked him for taking time to meet with me and reiterated when we'd meet next. He kept talking. I stood up and started moving towards the front hallway. He kept talking. Finally, I had to just say, "I'd like to spend more time with you, but I have another meeting I have to leave for now." I went to my hall closet and put my coat on; he either had to leave with me or sit alone in my kitchen!

I talked with some of my friends who also elected to leave corporate America and begin a consulting practice, either going solo or in partnership with someone else. I asked them how they manage the balance between work and having an actual life and I had some interesting responses which I'd like to share.

I know several female consultants who've found ways to balance work and family life. Here are some suggestions they've shared with me along the way:

- Schedule "play days" during the week once a month with a wonderful friend. Depending on the weather, the day might be spent going to an art museum, the zoo, or shopping. Quality, relaxing time together is important, not what you do.
- Take time in the morning for prayer and exercise before starting work. (I can hear you now, saying, but I don't have time for exercise! Yes, you do. You can take 5 minutes for deep breathing and stretching. Sure you can.)
- Limit nights out during the week to two: one for work and one for social activities.
- Take breaks at lunch to walk and recharge creative juices.
- Schedule regular working hours with real boundaries and practice time management techniques to actually stay within those boundaries.

Tina Macon has been a conflict resolution consultant for about three years and was a diversity consultant for several years before that time. She left industry in order to freely focus on the areas of HR management that she was passionate about. She does acknowledge that there have been times when she has regretted her decision, revolving around lulls in between contracts when income generation is slow. Mostly, though, she's happy as a consultant and takes these steps to balance her life:

- I have set better boundaries for myself and actually "walk away from work" after a certain time of day.

- My family is my number one priority and if what I'm doing interferes too greatly with that, then I let it go.
- I take time to pray, reflect, and be honest with myself about why I want to be a consultant.

Tina gives this advice to those of you considering the consulting field: align yourself with people who can help you and are willing to become a part of your support network (you will need it!). Stay current in your field and be flexible. See setbacks as growth opportunities and not failures.

Across these successful and talented women, we see a pattern. The key to building the balancing habit is setting—and sticking to—boundaries. Know what you want and "go for it," but know when it's time to step back and recharge your batteries. You can have more than two speeds (warp speed or off).

Another story of balance—moving between consulting and the corporate world—is shared here by our friend and colleague, Renee Springer.

BALANCING THE LIFE OF A CONSULTANT IN AND OUT OF CORPORATE AMERICA

By Renee Springer

As I reflect upon my experience I remember some very anxious moments when I was in corporate America trying to balance being a wife, mother, and student as well as running a household.

It was a challenging time. I often used the cliché that it wasn't, "the quantity of time that was important, it was the quality of time." So I carved out time in the evenings to do the cooking (sometimes), the homework, baths and storytelling. I remember thinking I had a pretty good routine going and thought I was "Super Woman" doing it all. I always kept my Saturdays for the girls, Friday evenings for my husband, and Sundays for my family. It seemed to work pretty well for several years and then the traveling for work 65 percent of the time, and extended late hours of work, and other outside activities trying to keep up took its toll.

I realized later, that you really *cannot* do it all and truly give it the right quality of time. Something always suffers. I thank God after the divorce I had the wherewithal to slow down, step back, and put things in the right perspective. I was a single parent and my options were limited in doing everything. I needed more flexibility than the corporate workplace provided. I needed to pick up the girls from school, attend the rehearsals and plays, go to piano lessons and/or soccer practice. Now, I had to find a "back up" for each of us to take on the duties with the kids.

In addition to the divorce, I was soon "downsized" for the first time in my career. I had decided I developed enough programs, established enough training and interventions that it was time to become a consultant. I traded the long hours in corporate America, and started my own business, with more flexibility in my time and work schedule (which, at times, still extended into nighttime). As a consultant and business owner, I learned to manage the work around normal hours during the day while the kids were at school, and do whatever else had to be done when they were asleep at night. I enjoyed the freedom and opportunity to be more a part of their lives at that time of their lives. My days were still long, but, it felt easier to spend time and work around their schedules rather than being tied to set hours and times like I had been in the corporate world.

As the children got older, and they drove themselves to their own activities, I had more time to do things that I wanted to do. I thought I might revisit the corporate life—what I had missed as a consultant was the camaraderie and collaboration that takes place inside a company with other colleagues. I had been an independent consultant and often worked alone. For me, I seemed to be less creative and innovative and felt stifled by the lack of sharing, and having someone to bounce things off. I'm a people person and truly missed the daily interactions with colleagues.

After returning to corporate America I'm more mature, more relaxed and not trying to change the world. I find it easier. My age makes me less frantic and stressed. I see things in a different perspective—it's a job and I am blessed to enjoy what I do. I don't play the politics the same way. They still exist, but I feel I have choices to play or not to play. Before I felt I had to play the politics and that was stressful. Today, my focus is on delivering what I do best. I am not concerned with climbing the ladder, I've climbed to the top of my profession. I have lots of experience and knowledge to offer and I stand on that. My role has expanded beyond my position, I see myself as a mentor and coach to others. I feel their respect and overall appreciation.

I have concluded that there is a time and place for each position, whether as a consultant or a corporate employee. Examine your skill set and life style to determine what's most important. Ultimately, having a strong spiritual foundation to trust and rely on God helped me in later years to reach the best balance for my family and for me.

TIPS AND TECHNIQUES: REBOUND TO BALANCE

We're going to look briefly at something we call The Habit of Balance. The Habit of Balance requires changing our behavior or attitude to rebound to balance, like re-setting the timer on our oven. Being in balance rather than out of balance becomes our status quo. The habit of rebounding to balance can become our new status quo. This habit asserts itself when a variety of factors cause imbalance in our lives.

We each have our challenges and our coping mechanisms. Sometimes our source of imbalance is *external*—like the tragedies of 9/11, Katrina, or massive floods, hurricanes and tornadoes. Sometimes the source is concern or worry about our family - it is *familial*—our close family member is serving in a war zone, our father is ill, our mother is in a retirement facility, our sons or daughters are using drugs. Sometimes, our imbalance is very *personal*—we are in a difficult marriage, we are in a job we hate, or we are going through menopause.

Each of these types of stressors is different and our coping mechanisms are different. Where our stress is very personal, we can sometimes change the situation and we need to try. Sometimes, for reasons that may be complicated by the familial or more external factors, we cannot change our personal situation—at least right now. When stress throws us out of balance, we may need the help of healthcare professionals—medical doctors, psychologists, or social workers to get us through a difficult period.

When we find a light—a vision for the future—and take just one small step toward that light, we begin the journey of a thousand steps toward a more balanced lifestyle – toward our Habit of Balance. We feel better when we have a sense of control. We can send money to the victims of Katrina; we can organize a letter writing campaign to our troops in harm's way; or we can give ourselves one night (or one hour) a week to remove ourselves from the reality of bad personal stuff.

We can alter our commitments to give ourselves more time for healing those things that hurt. We can play in the dirt or the water, exercise, watch funny movies, drink water, eat better, get more organized for a better time. We can make a list of the people and things for which we are grateful.

We can write notes to others who are having a hard time and bring ourselves back to equilibrium, by recognizing that our troubles could be much worse.

"Don't go around saying the world owes you a living. The world owes you nothing. It was here first."

—Mark Twain

≈

Remember what Albert Einstein said—light is the only constant—time and space are relative. When we ask ourselves: "Will this matter in five years" or "What is the worst thing that could happen?" we can sometimes talk ourselves to a less stressed and more balanced way of thinking. That attitude can result in behavior that will free us to resume A Habit of Balance.

14

Aha! Moments

"Doubt is the beginning, not the end, of wisdom."
—George Iles

≈

Terri

My first Aha! moment came when I heard Memory Ryan speak about Aha! moments in the mid-1970s. Before that time, I didn't know the experience had a name. Memory said that these were the moments of realization, when something clicked in our minds that said, "Yes, that is it. That is what I have been searching for."

≈

The sense of mental discovery when new information finds old information—be it data, thought, memory or feeling—and links it together is like magic. In reality, it is simply giving your brain time to sort the new information of your short-term memory into the buckets of data and information in your long-term memory. Sometimes this happens while you are awake, but even more often, it is when you sleep, thus the reason that many great minds in our history took naps during the day. The theory is that by sorting during a nap, there is more room in your short-term memory for new data.

APPLICATION

When I conduct training programs I use a bowl of paperclips to demonstrate the learning that is possible in the session. I show the participants the bowl of colored paperclips, give them a small dish and ask them to take some clips. I ask the participants to choose the items most relevant to them —that they can use the clips to mark the pages to remember the idea later. Of course, not all items will be relevant to each person. The participants can choose the items they want to remember and what reaches them. I then take a paperclip and describe to them how these paperclips can be strung together when learning takes place, when something is triggered in their brain about how the new information we are learning ties to something they already know. I show a picture of the bowl and linked paperclips on the screen to further reinforce the idea. Touching and seeing the paperclips as well as hearing the process described appeals to those individuals who use disparate and multiple sources of intelligence as their learning method.

The bowl is set in the middle of the table, so that they can easily reach for more during the session if they so choose.

When they choose only three or four paperclips and do not reach for more in the session, I know they are not in the right frame of mind to learn today.

GETTING READY FOR "AHA!" MOMENTS

"Specific patterns of brain activity precede "Aha!" moments of insight and suggest that preparing mentally to think creatively may help in problem solving" indicates a WebMD Medical News review of a June, 2006 study in Psychological Science. The actual publication goes on to note:

> Mark Jung-Beeman, a cognitive neuroscientist at Northwestern University, showed that distinct brain areas contribute when people solve problems with insight, that is, when solutions are accompanied by 'Aha!' moments. The patterns of brain activity suggest an increase in 'top-down' processing, and increased contributions from the brain's right hemisphere.

Beeman attributed the latter effect to the more diffuse links in the right brain, which allow for novel or idiosyncratic connections across distantly related concepts.

John Kounious, a cognitive neuroscientist at Drexel University, showed that, although the final moment of insight is sudden, there are substantial changes in brain activity leading up to insight solutions to problems, such as a quieting of the sensory areas of the brain in the seconds before the solution reaches consciousness. He interpreted these results as the unconscious brain searching for solutions, but having to quiet down external inputs to bring a candidate solution into consciousness. Moreover, patterns of brain activity before people even see a problem predict whether they will solve that problem with insight, or more analytically. Finally, he also reports that moderate rates of arousal are best for problem solving, with the optimal amount of arousal being lower as problems become more difficult.

Teresa Amabile, a psychologist at Harvard Business School, discussed how emotions can influence the creative process. Amabile found a consistent, positive relationship between positive emotion and creativity.

She showed that positive affect preceded creativity in the coming days. She also found that having a new idea or insight can evoke immediate (though short-lived) feelings of elation—even when the idea is a relatively minor one. Amabile's study revealed a connection between positive emotion and creativity at work.[53]

More recently, a Harvard Medical School study[54] indicated that laughter experienced just prior to a learning activity increased the potential for that Aha! moment to occur.

In short, affect and laughter are important precursors to Aha! moments.

CLIENT SURPRISES

In October 2007, I was teaching a half-day seminar on teambuilding to a diverse group of individuals from different companies. They were in the midst of a training exercise called Blind Squares. Each person in a group holds onto a rope and forms a rough circle; then, each is blindfolded; no talking is permitted. They are told to form the rope circle into a square.

As background, the leadership of that group had not been consistent—they were all leaders—the number two or three in their organizations. The leadership had rotated among several in the group prior to this exercise.

After the group became entangled in the rope and a square was nowhere to be seen, I asked them to remove the blindfold and see what had happened.

I asked them to proceed to form a square a second time; this time they were permitted to talk and remove their blindfolds. An interesting dynamic ensued.

During this second exercise, one of the participants retained the blindfold. He began to provide verbal direction to the group. The others followed his direction, and no one told him that he was the only one still wearing a blindfold. In short order, they formed a square.

In debriefing the exercise, I asked the blindfolded leader how he felt when he learned he was the only person with a blindfold on. He seemed a bit embarrassed—until one of the other members spoke up. "He seemed to know what he was doing. He had a vision; we could tell he was following the picture in his mind. We could all see that he was proceeding in a way that was going to help us get the results. It didn't seem necessary to tell him he was wearing a blindfold when we weren't." Affirming heads nodded around the room.

People continue to amaze me and surprise me after all these years. I have personally been through this exercise numerous times and conducted the exercise with numerous groups. This was a first for this outcome.

The group was proud of itself; the leader was proud of himself.

nda

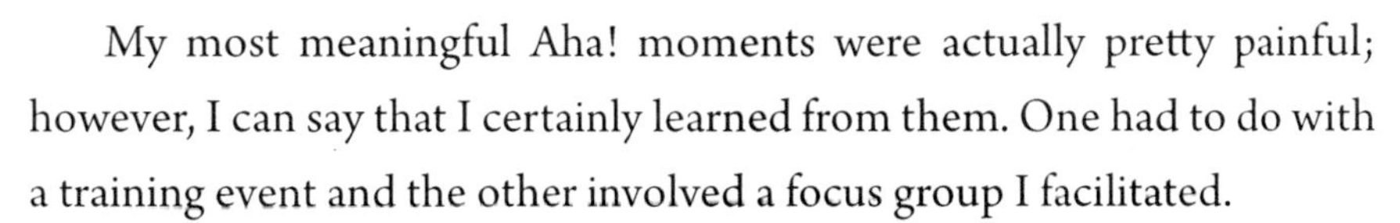
My most meaningful Aha! moments were actually pretty painful; however, I can say that I certainly learned from them. One had to do with a training event and the other involved a focus group I facilitated.

In my first year of consulting, I began facilitating occasional workshops for a local university. The person who recruited me to do this was the director of the university's consulting group and an educator for whom I have a high level of respect. So when he suggested to me, after a few workshops, that I learn to balance lecture and activities more effectively *and* be more diligent about providing breaks to participants, I was embarrassed. He was absolutely right, of course. I'm what researcher Kolb describes as an "abstract conceptualizer," which means I'm perfectly content listening to a professor or trainer that I believe is a knowledgeable lecturer about a topic that interests me. I don't feel the need to be entertained by fun activities or role plays. I don't feel the need to share my stories with other participants in workshops. My mentor helped me have an Aha! moment . . . just because I don't have that need doesn't mean others don't. When my mentor had to pull me aside after reading yet another set of evaluations that indicated "too much lecture" and tell me this (very tactfully), I was embarrassed. I love being a teacher and this is my primary motivation; and admittedly, I enjoy the status of being someone with knowledge that perhaps others don't have. I was crushed to discover that not everyone wanted to hear what I knew and had to say —at least not in the form of a lecture.

My mentor's comments stuck, though. I build interactive segments into every workshop I facilitate. Now, twenty years later, feedback on my workshops always includes statements like, "excellent use of interactive tools" and, "great opportunity to participate and get involved in discussions." I time myself when I'm preparing to facilitate workshops and do not ever spend more than five minutes at a time "lecturing."

A couple of years after my training epiphany, a client asked if I would facilitate a few focus groups with the objective of obtaining candid feedback about the top leadership's management style. My mission was to solicit feedback to pass along to the leadership team, and to make recommendations for that team's professional development. I thought, as the senior person asked me to take on this project, "Well, isn't that nice that the lead team wants to hear from their employees."

I discovered what they wanted to hear from their employees. They did not, however, want to hear negative comments from their employees! After the focus groups, which I thought went very well, I compiled the results and my recommendation for action steps to enhance relationships between management and employees. The feedback wasn't all rosy;

however, it was relatively positive compared to what I'd seen from other organizations. I sent the feedback and my report in writing to the lead team so they could digest it before we met a few days later. On my way to the meeting, the senior person called me on my cell to give me a "heads up" that her crew was pretty doggone angry. They thought the feedback was unfair, too critical, and too one-sided without enough positive comments. They thought I must be at fault for letting the focus groups "spiral out of control" and become venting sessions against a perfectly nice and wonderful leadership team.

When I arrived at the company, I got a very cool reception from the senior person. She abruptly ushered me into the meeting room, where I found myself facing about eight sets of accusing eyes. I was mortified and a flood of questions overcame me! I started to doubt myself. Had I mishandled the focus groups? Should I have softened the feedback through a different lens? Thankfully, I kept my composure and immediately snapped back to reality, though. I couldn't whitewash peoples' candid feedback to diffuse the message, or this group of managers wouldn't be compelled to act. I wouldn't have done the job they asked me to do.

I attempted to calm down the lead team by comparing their results with those of similar organizations. They finally said, "We have some work to do, but this doesn't sound nearly as bad as we reacted to initially." The others soon realized that, all things considered, their feedback was pretty good and that improving relationships between themselves and employees would not be an impossible task. The session ended well, but I was sweating bullets . . . and I learned that I didn't want to take on this type of assignment ever again.

LESSONS LEARNED

- You can prepare yourself for Aha! moments.
- Preparing for Aha! moments is just another good reason for increasing the laughter in your day.
- Naps can actually improve information acquisition and memory.
- Clients will continue to surprise you.
- Good clients provide positive and useful feedback.
- Consulting isn't easy, but it is worthwhile and rewarding.

15

"War Stories"—A Consultant's Reality

We have learned a few things as consultants:

1. Every day is an adventure.
2. You have to keep your sense of humor.
3. We are grateful for every day we get to do this thing called consulting, because we are both passionate about it, it is fun and frustrating, and we can make a living at it.

Neither of us would want to do anything else.

GYPSY

Terri

In my fourteenth year of operations, I arrived at my retail client's store and was ushered in by the owner's daughter, and her dog, Tucker. Tucker and I are friends by now. The client and I have been working together for three years.

As usual, the owner, Joy has a few details to handle before we begin. This time, a last minute client is coming in for a fitting and she needs to take care of this before we begin the strategy session to cover *time management*. She apologizes, as she always does, and I just laugh. This is standard operating procedure.

She has to do the fitting in the back parking lot because her client is a horse. (Well, the client is the owner of the horse, but the horse is getting the fitting.) A small horse, a three year old named Gypsy. Gypsy reluctantly jumps out of the trailer (pushed by her owner), and immediately, happy to be on solid ground, stands perfectly still once led to her "standing place." She is patient while the costume designer puts the pattern in place, slipping it over her head and adding the girth under her middle - the belt has to be fitted as well.

GYPSY'S FIRST FITTING FOR THE FISH COSTUME

Gypsy is going to the County Fair, with her owner's four-year-old grandson. The little boy is going as Huck Finn and Gypsy is going as a fish. In her bright blue satin lamé costume with vivid purple sequined fins, she will be a sight for summer eyes. The Costumer Designer fusses with the costume's fins, until it makes me squirm, but Gypsy stands still for it. Finally, forty-five minutes later, the fish costume is fitted and Gypsy returns to her trailer. In a week, Gypsy will return for her final fitting.

The costume shop owner has now opened up an entirely new market—Custom Costumes for Special Pets. The summer is her slowest quarter for her business and now, she has discovered a new market niche to fill that time. Never underestimate the resourcefulness of a small business owner!

FINAL FITTING WITH THE DESIGNER

(See what I mean by "always an adventure?")

KEEPING YOUR SENSE OF HUMOR

What we do as consultants is serious business and we need to treat it that way. However, that does not mean we have to take ourselves seriously.

THE COCKTAIL PARTY AND THE NEW SHOES

Terri

So, the new shoes were a little big. I decided to put the insoles in the shoes for a more comfortable fit. As usual, before a big event, I was dressed to the nines, make-up and hair as perfect as possible, and with great confidence, I left for the Club.

I was meeting some potential clients and they had not arrived, so I moved around the room with ease at this city club's membership party. As a Board Member, it was my responsibility to make certain that everyone was mingling. I said hello to old friends and chatted with new prospects for the club. After all, the purpose of a party is for the guests to talk to the other guests.

Soon my guests arrived and I chatted with them, introduced them to several other Board Members and guests. I then took them around the Club—providing the usual tour of all the facilities. They were prospects for my business and for club membership.

The evening went well—the second touch for the prospects was successful. I smiled as I left the Club for the parking lot to get my car. As I exited the elevator, I glanced down to avoid falling over the elevator threshold. As I walked off the elevator and into the parking lot, anyone seeing me would have thought I was crazy. Standing alone in the parking lot, I got lost in giggles. The insoles in the shoes had worked their way out of the open-toed shoes and were flapping as I walked. For three minutes I stood in the parking lot, unable to move, because I was laughing so hard.

I still don't know if anyone noticed. If they did, they didn't say anything. Sometimes you just have to laugh at yourself!

Post Script: There was a time when I would have been horrified at the thought of anyone seeing me with insoles flapping in the wind; one a half inch, the other an inch and one- half. But I have learned that while you have to take your <u>work</u> seriously, you can't take <u>yourself</u> too seriously.

≈

WE GET TO DO THIS, BUT IT IS SERIOUS WORK

A close friend shared with me that a Big 5 Consulting firm was brought in to her former employer to improve the operations. This firm was number one in their market but losing margins and wanted to improve. The consultant recommended significant facility changes including a major expansion consisting of building new super-warehouse and distribution facilities and closing down numerous local distribution centers. The consulting firm neglected to recognize that flexibility and fast delivery were important to client's customer as well as the fact that the firm was not in the distribution business, they were in the business of providing their customers with the product quickly, even if only a portion of the order could be filled.

That client took the recommendation of the consultant because they were one of the Big 5; the solution had worked for another of their clients.

The client is now in a survival mode, losing major market share and is hampered by the costs of conversion. Their pricing strategy had to be altered to cover the new facility capital expenses. Their market share has dropped—they are now fifth in the market share hierarchy of suppliers.

When you make a recommendation as a consultant, you bear the responsibility, not for the implemented results, but for a solid recommendation that will work for the client in their environment and in their market. If you are not certain, then you need to tell the client the pros and cons of the recommendation and ask if they believe it will work.

Another time when it is important to be serious is when a client breaks down in tears.

TEARS

One of the twenty participants in the training program on "Creating a New Job Description"—a quiet participant who had said little—burst into tears!

"What? What?" was my first thought. "What in the world?" We were using the previous training in Teambuilding with this group to design a new job description for the organization. All full-time employees were participating. We were in the middle of identifying the responsibilities of the job. What was tearful about that?

That is what I thought, not what I said.

As I mentioned previously, I am prone to calm in a crisis, so my automatic response kicked into action. I had been standing in front of the group—long table of handouts behind me. I immediately walked to the side of the room where the sobbing employee was seated and sat back on the table behind me. I closed out the rest of the group and focused my entire attention on the woman with the tears streaming down her face.

"Tell me about the tears," I said quietly and gently. I called her by name and just waited for a response. Through her sobs, she finally managed to get out some words that were not very coherent. Everyone else in the room sat so quietly that a dropped pin could be heard. After a couple more softly probing questions, I managed to learn that she was concerned others felt she was not doing her job, and therefore the organization was creating this new job. Her real concern was that her job would be eliminated after this one was created. Once she slowed the racking motion of her body up and down from the emotion, I called for a break. The remaining participants slowly and quietly left the room.

The Executive Director and I talked with her individually during that break and she opted to leave the group for the remainder of the session. We did assure her that her perception was not the intent at all, but an attempt to actually relieve her of some of the responsibilities, so that she could indeed do her job better. It was to help her and not to hurt her. We thought we had made this clear in the beginning of the session.

Perhaps I should have seen this coming. But since it was a surprise to everyone, including the Director, I just chalked it up to experience and moved on to complete the job. That was nearly ten years ago now. Of course, now I do look for any signs of such emotion when working with any group for any purpose. Nothing like it has happened since.

Linda

MORE WAR STORIES

Any consultant has war stories, I suppose, and I'm no different. I've had some humorous experiences, some serious experiences, and some just plain weird experiences. All of these incidents have helped me grow personally and professionally and develop a healthy sense of humor. Let me share some of them with you.

In 2005, I was asked to conduct a sexual harassment investigation, something I do three or four times a year for clients. The impact of this particular investigation was huge because the "alleged perp" was a top executive with the company. After doing thorough interviews with witnesses and the person making the allegations, I met with the man who was the subject of the investigation. When I laid out the results of my interviews with everyone involved, I asked for his perspective. Usually, when I'm at this point with a person accused of sexual harassment, they're pretty upset and want to forcefully deny harassment of any type. In this case, the man leaned across the table, put his hand over mine, and said, "Honey, I know you women like to get attention. I'm just giving you what you want." I pulled my hand away, looked him straight in the eye and said, "Most of 'us women' want simply to be treated with respect. How would you like it if someone put their hands on your wife or daughter?" Typically, people get the point when I make a statement like this. Not our guy. His retort was, "My wife and daughter are ugly. They'd probably love to get some male attention." To make a long story short, I ended up recommending that this fellow be terminated because he had a looooooooooong history of harassing behavior and he steadfastly refused to acknowledge how unacceptable this was in the workplace. He actually brought his wife to the termination hearing and asked to bring her into the meeting, saying that he had nothing to hide! (I asked her to wait in the lobby.)

In 2006, I had my first challenge to a fight. Since I'm 5'2 ½" tall and weigh 119 in full winter gear, I don't exactly project the image of a person that's accustomed to fighting. Here's what happened. I was facilitating an employee meeting for a client company in the manufacturing arena. During the meeting, I asked employees to work with others at their table for several breakout activities. During these activities, I walked around the room to provide guidance to groups that were slightly off course or had questions about what they were supposed to do. As I walked by one table, it was clear that the group was definitely engaged in the activity but was not carrying out the assigned task. I pulled out a chair, sat down, and asked if I could have their attention for a moment so I could clarify the assignment. The woman in the chair next to me was close to six feet tall, stocky, and loud. She had been loud and opinionated all day. She grabbed my wrist and said, "We're doing OK just the way we are. Leave us alone to finish." I smiled, gently pulled her hand from my wrist and placed it on the table. Before I could comment, one of the fellows at the table said, "Hey, Dr. Linda is a martial arts expert! I wouldn't mess with her." To this, my "buddy" said, "I can take you. Right here, right now." Whew! I'm not in the habit of fighting with clients or their employees. My response was to say that I wasn't interested in a fist fight but I was interested in making certain that this group was prepared to report out in 15 minutes with results that were on target, so they wouldn't be embarrassed in front of their peers and managers. The other people at the table, God love them, all said at about the same time, "Let's move on . . . what do we need to do?" I provided the clarification, got them on track, and moved to another table. During lunch break, the woman came up to me and said that she figured I had "ratted her out" to the boss by now. I told her that I didn't intend to do that, however I did expect not to *ever* hear of her doing anything like that again. (I haven't.)

Some of my training experiences are really fun, even with serious topics. Occasionally I do training on preventing sexual and racial harassment, always with a colleague. The first time I asked my colleague, Bill, to facilitate a series of sexual harassment workshops with me he agreed right away. I told him that we'd be doing some role plays to demonstrate what constitutes sexual harassment and that HE would be the person being harassed. He still agreed, and we did the planning with a loose script for the role plays. During the first role play for the first session, I wanted the audience and Bill to be surprised that 1) a professional looking person such as me could be guilty of harassment and 2) a person being harassed can really feel demeaned and embarrassed. In the script, I was supposed to lightly run my fingers up and down Bill's arm as I was standing next to him while discussing a report. I did that, then started playing with his tie, then I locked my arm through his. Bill was totally flustered, and the 40 men in the audience were clearly uncomfortable. Good . . . that was exactly what I wanted. I wanted them all to feel what it's like to be in that position, not to just read or hear about it. Bill told me on the flight back to Cincinnati that in the future he'd never take anyone's allegations of harassment lightly.

MORE SHOES

Well, I have a shoe and a client-in-tears story, too. I'll start with the shoe story. Three years ago, I was invited to have breakfast with an executive team for a national company, in their executive dining room. They were exploring the possibility of my doing some long-term projects with them. I had done some reading about the company and knew that the culture would be ultra conservative, traditional, and mostly male. The day of my meeting was cold, windy, and there were two inches of snow on the ground. Snow in Cincinnati is not unusual, but this was October, and the snowfall was not predicted. My dilemma was that the conservative, tailored suit I planned to wear would not look right with the muk-muks I typically wore on snowy days. My meeting was at 8:00 a.m. so there was no opportunity to shop for the type of boots that would be right for the skirt suit I was wearing. I couldn't walk through an unplowed parking lot in heels, and I didn't know if I'd have a private place (or time) to change into regular shoes before the executive team representative came to collect me from the lobby. So I opted to wear what I hoped would be a smart choice: high heeled black ankle boots that I could keep on during the meeting. I arrived at the company and was whisked away to the meeting seconds after I signed in. As I walked through the slippery tile hallways in my three inch heels, I glanced at other people I passed by. Everyone, male or female, had on a corporate uniform, which included sensible shoes. I got more than one backward look at my high heeled, trendy boots. I walked into the dining room and most of the (all male) team I was meeting with was already seated . . . sitting there in their Brooks Brothers suits and wingtips. My thinking was that I should just get myself seated as soon as possible so they could focus on my otherwise conservative attire. But no, my guide took me by the elbow and steered me around the table to individually meet each person. Every single one of them looked at my boots. That whole doggoned meeting I was thinking about my boots and the bad impression they must've made. At the end of the meeting, the CEO said, "Linda, I think you would really spice things up around here! When can we begin our project together?" Who knew?!

MORE TEARS

It's always disconcerting when a client breaks into tears, whether it's in a private meeting with just the two of you or in a group setting. Not that it should make a difference, but for me it's more painful when it's a guy getting teary eyed—maybe because it's so unexpected. I was assisting an executive with some long-term planning, and we were in his office surrounding by files and stacks of paperwork. He was stretched pretty thin with work and I knew he hadn't had a good night's sleep or spent quality time with his family in months. During the meeting, he commented that he hadn't seen much of his kids lately. He said this in between bites of a boiled egg, which was his lunch. I asked him who he believed was in charge of this state of affairs. He paused for a very long moment. Tears welled up in his eyes. He finally said, "That would be me." So I asked him if he wanted to take a few minutes to brainstorm some ideas on work-life balance. He did. But he took a few minutes first to go collect himself in the washroom. I had to take a few deep breaths myself while he was gone so I could be composed to work objectively with him, bless his heart. He is a lot more balanced now, several months later . . . and his wife sent me flowers about two weeks after that meeting!

rri

IN SUMMARY

Like every other aspect of operating in the 21st century, the work of a consultant is collaborative. Consulting is collaborative effort between the client and the consultant. The time has passed that the consultant is always right and the client is always wrong (if that were ever the case). Collaborative solutions, where the consultant and client discuss the options, the pros and cons, the impact of the recommendations are the current norm. Command and control is being eliminated in the vast majority of solidly performing operations. Transparency is the key to successful endeavors.

I advise my clients to tell me if something about the recommendation is uncomfortable. When it is uncomfortable, I urge them to discover why, then we talk through it. Change only takes place on the edge of discomfort.

A good consultant improves the situation, by her presence and her work. A good consultant concentrates on the client, among distractions, to listen, and to learn quickly the complexities of the organization and the issue at hand, to come prepared with care, tools and techniques that work, to go away with the issue satisfactorily resolved, and to do this with the collaborative involvement of the client.

Terri

Linda

CONCLUSION

We get to do it—this thing called consulting.

Neither of us can think of a better job than the one we have. We both love our clients, we love what we do and we love our bosses. Neither can we think of a better profession for women. Women make the best salespeople and we think, with some few male exceptions, that women make the better consultants. We listen, we empathize, we want our clients to be successful and toward that end we do everything we can to make them successful.

We hate it when they forget to call us to tell us what happened. We hate it when we know it is the right thing to do and they don't take our advice (the first time).

We hate it when something catastrophic happens and they can't continue to do what they love.

We collaborate, we cajole, we care. In general, we are a pretty considerate and consensus building lot, we women. We hope you will join us in consulting or create your own journey.

If you want to determine your aptitude for this business, then refer to our chapter eleven where you will find access to a site that will provide you with an analysis of your aptitude.

And, whatever you decide, good luck on your journey. It has been a pleasure sharing ours with you.

END NOTES

1. *The Woman Entrepreneur,* Robert D. Hisrich, Candida G. Brush, D.C. Heath and Company, 1986.
2. Small Business Profile, Kentucky and Ohio, U.S. Small Business Administration, Office of Advocacy, February 2011. www.sba.gov/advo.
3. Introduction to the Consulting Industry, Trend Overview, Consulting Market Research - statistics, Plunkett Research,® Ltd. www.plunkettresearch.com (retrieved August 2011).
4. Consulting Industry, Statistic Overview, Plunkett Research,® Ltd. www.plunkettresearch.com (retrieved August 2011).
5. SBA.gov Office of Advocacy's Research and Statistics. Website information, (retrieved May 27, 2011) under Frequently Asked Questions, How Important are Small Businesses to the U.S. Economy?
6. Ibid.
7. *Small Business Resource Guide for the 110th Congress,* National Federation of Independent Business, November 2007.
8. *Kauffman Index of Entrepreneurial Activity 1996-2010,* March 2011. www.kauffman.org.

9. "After Inception: How Enduring is Job Creation by Start-ups?" August 2010. Michael Horrell and Robert Litan, Ewing Marion Kauffman Foundation 2010.
10. "Why Your Start-Up Will Fail," Forbes.com, Wil Schroter, September 24, 2007.
11. *The Woman Entrepreneur*, Robert D. Hisrich and Candida G. Brush, Lexington Books, Macmillian, Inc., 1986.
12. "The Small Business Economy, For the Data Year 2005, Report to the President", Small Business Administration, December, 2006.
13. Ibid.
14. National Federation of Independent Business, Small Business Resource Guide, 2011.
15. Ibid.
16. Ibid
17. www.sba.gov/advocacy. September 2011. For an additional source, see NFIB Small Business Resource Guide, where the numbers are 60-80 percent.
18. Angels are individual investors. The word was first used for financial supporters of Broadway plans, but now generally applies to individual investors.
19. *The World is Flat*, Thomas L. Friedman. Farrar, Straus and Giroux, 2005.
20. *How to Life Your Dreams and Love Your Life Ladies Who Launch Embracing Entrepreneurship & Creativity As a Lifestyle*, Victoria Colligan and Beth Schoenfeldt, with Amy Swift, St. Martin Press, New York, 2007.
21. "The Coming Entrepreneurial Boom", June, 2009. www.kauffman.org (search for FastFacts).
22. National Federation of Independent Business, Small Business Resource Guide, 2011.
23. Business Wire News Release, authored by Yahoo! March, 2008.
24. Make Mine a Million $ Business is a program of Count Me In for Women's Economic Independence — and founding partner, OPEN from American Express®.
25. *The World is Flat*, Thomas L. Friedman. Farrar, Straus and Giroux (2005).
26. "The Coming Entrepreneurial Boom", June, 2009. www.kauffman.org (search for FastFacts).
27. Ibid.
28. "The Kauffman Firm Survey", March 2008. www.kauffman.org (search for FastFacts).

29. *The World is Flat,* Thomas L. Friedman. Farrar, Straus and Giroux, 2005.

30. "The Making of an Expert", Harvard Business Review, July-August, 2007.

31. Ibid.

32. Ibid.

33. *The Entrepreneurial Mind,* Jeffery A. Timmons. Brickhouse Publishing Company, March 1989.

34. The Urban Learning Center is a Northern Kentucky community initiative designed to reach and fund inner-city adults in their quest for education beyond high school. Over 90 percent of the participants reached in the first seven years were women, who are the key to their children achieving additional education. Funding consists of books, tuition, and fees, child care, pencils and paper and transportation if necessary. The investment required of the individual attending these classes is $10 per person per class.

35. Plunkett Research®, Ltd. www.plunkettresearch.com/consulting.

36. Global Consulting Marketplace 2010-2013, Trends, Profiles and Forecasts, Kennedy Consulting Research & Advisory.

37. "The Economic Future Just Happened", June 2009. www.kauffman.org (search for FastFacts).

38. More information on generic consulting labels and definitions is found in the work of Peter Block, in *Flawless Consulting,* 2000.

39. Angel investors normally provide less than $500,000 in funds plus business expertise and industry contacts to help a young firm. Sometimes they actively participate in the operation of the business.

40. *Angel Investing . . .* Mark Van Osnabrugge and Robert J. Robinson, and "How to Be an Angel" by Daniel Kadlec, http://www.time.com/time/magazine/article/0,9171,476408,00.html

41. "Will a Stranger Lend You $25,000?" John Tozzi, 2008 BusinessWeek Online, May 6, 2008.

42. www.sba.gov/advocacy (Retrieved May, 2011). "How Important are small businesses to the U. S. economy?" and "Startup Business Characteristics and Dynamics: A Data Analysis of the Kauffman Firm Survey," An Office of Advocacy Working Paper, Small Business Administration, Office of Advocacy, 2009.

43. *Smart Start Your Kentucky Business,* (available for each state), The Oasis Press,© 1997, Chapter Two – Your Business Structure.

44. "From Welfare to Work for African American Women", A dissertation submitted to the Division of Research and Advance Studies of the University of Cincinnati, Michael J. Posey, Ed.D., 2000.

45. *How to Life Your Dreams and Love Your Life Ladies Who Launch Embracing Entrepreneurship & Creativity As a Lifestyle,* Victoria Colligan and Beth Schoenfeldt, with Amy Swift, St. Martin Press, New York, 2007.

46. *Stress: Living and Working in a Changing World.* George Manning, Kent Curtis, and Steve McMillen, Whole Person Associates, 1999.

47. I like to give credit where credit is due. However, this only slightly modified document was forwarded to me by a recruiter some years ago. There are no copyrights or other distinguishing notes on the document for me to trace this back to the author.

48. *Value-Based Fees How to Charge – and Get – What You're Worth,* Alan Weiss, Pfeiffer, San Francisco, CA, 2002.

49. ENT: Innovation and Entrepreneurship, Northern Kentucky University, Fifth Third Entrepreneurship Program for a course entitled Innovation and Entrepreneurship, textbook: *Innovation and the General Manager,* Clayton Christianson, Harvard Press.

50. *How to Life Your Dreams and Love Your Life Ladies Who Launch Embracing Entrepreneurship & Creativity As a Lifestyle,* Victoria Colligan and Beth Schoenfeldt, with Amy Swift, St. Martin Press, New York, 2007.

51. *How to Life Your Dreams and Love Your Life Ladies Who Launch Embracing Entrepreneurship & Creativity As a Lifestyle,* Victoria Colligan and Beth Schoenfeldt, with Amy Swift, St. Martin Press, New York, 2007.

52. "Flex-Options Guide, Creating 21st Century Workplace Flexibility", A Project of the U.S. Department of Labor, Women's Bureau, developed by Linda Roundtree, Roundtree Consulting LLC and Karen Kerrigan, Women Entrepreneur's Inc., February, 2007.

53. "Linda Kerber, Women of the Republic: Intellect and Ideology in Revolutionary America", 1980. http://videri.wikidot.com/kerberrepublic.

54. Often quoted, but we can only locate tertiary source for this statement.

55. "New ideas about new ideas. (Conferences)," NBER Reporter, June 22, 2006. National Bureau of Economic Research, Inc.

Appendix 1

Bibliography of First Read Books for Small Business Owners

Top Five Books for Start-up Companies

Think and Grow Rich, Napoleon Hill. (old book, timeless ideas, mindset)

Smart Start Your (state) Business, Oasis Press

Running A One-Person Business, Claude Whitmyer and Salli Rasberry.

The E-Myth, Revisited , Michael E. Gerber

Seven Habits of Highly Effective People, Steven Covey

Next Five Books

Get Everyone in Your Boat and Rowing in the Same Direction, Bob Boylan (managing your operation)

Good to Great, Jim Collins (creating your organization)

Guerilla Marketing, Jay Conrad Levinson (marketing your organization)

Dig Your Well Before You Are Thirsty, Harvey Mackay. (networking and client management)

All I Really Need to Know I Learned in Kindergarten, Robert Fulghum

The Next Five Books

The Eighth Habit, Steven Covey.

First, Break All the Rules, Marcus Buckingham and Curt Coffman

The Tipping Point, Malcolm Gladwell

Blink, Malcolm Gladwell

Empowerment Takes More Than a Minute, Ken Blanchard, John P. Carlos, Alan Randolph

Advanced Reading

Now, Discover Your Strengths, Marcus Buckingham & Donald O. Clifton, Ph.D.

The World is Flat, Thomas L. Friedman

The Art of Leadership, George Manning and Kent Curtis

How to Talk to Anyone, Anytime, Anywhere: The Secrets of Good Communication, Larry King.

Building Community: The Human Side of Work, George Manning, Steve McMillan, Kent Curtis.

Innovation and Entrepreneurship, Peter F. Drucker.

Mastering the Rockefeller Habits, Verne Harnish.

The Prince, Machiavelli (look for the philosophy of managing money)

The Hidden Agenda (old but relevant to the hidden way that things take place in organizations)

The Age of Unreason, Charles Handy.

The Speed of Trust, Steven Covey, Jr.

Raising the Bar: A Handbook for Managers on Innovation, Creativity and Continuous Improvement, Alan Weiss

Very Advanced Reading

Innovation and the General Manager, Clayton M. Christensen (textbook, difficult to read, but concepts not as yet found in a more readable format)

A Whole New Mind, Daniel H. Pink

Management of the Absurd, Richard Farson.

The Capitalist Philosophers, Andrea Gabor

The Art of War, Sun Tzu

The Art of War for Women, Chin-Ning Chu

Leadership and the New Science, Margaret Wheatley.

The Abilene Paradox, Jerry B. Harvey (management, group think and ethics)

Freakonomics, Steven D. Levitt and Stephen J. Dubner

Any Charles Handy book

Any Guy Kawasaki book

Any Alan Weiss book

Any George Manning book

Consulting

Consultant's Calling, Geoffrey M. Bellman

Million Dollar Consulting, Alan Weiss

Flawless Consulting, Peter Block

Million Dollar Consulting Toolkit, Alan Weiss

The Computer Consultant's Guide, Janet Ruhl

Ladies Who Launch, Victoria Colligan and Beth Schoenfeldt

Value-Based Fees, Alan Weiss

Recommended reading lists provided by Terri Bonar-Stewart, Just The Basics®

Appendix 2

Potential Client Log

Date of Initial Call: ____

Taken By: ____

Company Name: ____

Address: ____

Company Contact: ____

Title: ____

Project Description: ____

____

____

____

____

Project Objectives: ____

____

____

____

____

Target Start Date: ____

Target Completion: ____

Action Steps:

____Consultation meeting set with potential client on ______________

____Potential client referred to ______________________________

____Other ____

Appendix 3

Sample Proposal

Gravett and Associates
P.O. Box 54429
Cincinnati, OH 45254

(513)753-8870
Fax: (513)753-8391
www.gravett.com

Proposal For

____

OBJECTIVES: Expand and enhance the efforts of the Diversity and Member Development Team to help staff have a deeper understanding and appreciation of diversity and better serve the Company during change.

PHASE I: **GAIN UNDERSTANDING OF COMPANY'S NEEDS TO SUPPORT DIVERSITY EFFORTS**

Step 1:

Develop a tailored Culture Audit to assess staff's perspectives on recruiting, orientation, training, and development across all demographic groups. Dr. Gravett will develop a draft culture audit for Diversity and Member Development Team's review and input.

Time Frame: Draft instrument will be developed within one week from acceptance of Proposal and returned to Team for review. Final instrument will be completed within one week after Team input.

As the Culture Audit is being developed, Team will review and finalize Purpose Statement for distribution to staff at the time of the Culture Audit distribution.

Step 2:

Dr. Gravett will meet with staff in break-outs to explain, with a Diversity and Member Development Team member, how the Culture Audit process works and how the results will be used. The Culture Audit will be distributed during these break-outs and can be completed and sent to Dr. Gravett in stamped, self-addressed envelopes or the instrument can be completed anonymously online.

Time Frame: Staff is provided with a 10-day deadline to complete and return the Culture Audit.

Step 3:

Dr. Gravett will compile and synthesize the results of the Culture Audit, capturing themes from comments and determining patterns across demographic groups such as training and development needs for staff in entry-level positions. She may recommend that focus groups be conducted for specific groups to solicit ideas and suggestions for meeting the needs of those groups more effectively.

Time Frame: Culture Audit results will be compiled and summarized within 10 days after the deadline for return to Dr. Gravett. Focus groups will be facilitated within two weeks after the summary of results.

Step 4: Dr. Gravett will compile the results of the focus groups, if conducted, and prepare written recommendations for the Diversity and Member Development Team. She will send the recommendations in written form and then meet with the Team to discuss an action plan and timeline.

Time Frame: The written recommendations will be completed within 10 days after the final focus group or deadline for Culture Audit completion. Dr. Gravett will meet with the Team to discuss an action plan within 30 days after sending the written recommendations.

Cost for Phase I: Meetings with Team at hourly rate of $ X /hour.

Development of Culture Audit; Distribution; Compilation of **Results:** $ X /completed instrument.

Focus Group Facilitation at hourly rate of $ X /hour.

Development of Written Recommendations: $ X .

PHASE II: **ACTION PLAN DEVELOPMENT**

Dr. Gravett will meet with Team to review written recommendations and brainstorm a specific action plan with events, timeline, success criteria, process checkpoints, and cost.

Cost for Phase II: Meeting with Team at hourly rate of $ X /hour.

PHASE III: ACTION PLAN IMPLEMENTATION AND MAINTENANCE

Step 1: Develop and facilitate a tailored training event around the Myers-Briggs Type Indicator for all staff. This is a one full day or two half-day training event. MBTI instruments are distributed and scored by Dr. Gravett in advance of the training. (Cost is $95 per packet of 10.)

Step 2: Steps 2 forward will be decided during the Action Plan Development in Phase II of the process, as well as a specific timeline for process checkpoints.

This proposal can be tailored for any phase to meet the changing needs of the organization.

Appendix 4

Categories of Expertise
Detailed Example: Field of Human Resources

We have used human resources as an example in most situations because that is what we both know best. The categories will be the same for any consulting field: level of expertise, range of products and services provided, and specific products and services. The detail provided below is specific to our field.

An example in the field of Human Resources:

1. Your level of expertise
   a. Compensation specialist
   b. Generalist
   c. Recruiter
2. Range of products and services provided:
   a. By product line
   b. By service line

3. Specific products and services:
    a. Executive compensation, sales compensation, wage and salary administration plans
    b. Sales recruiter? Food and beverage industry recruiter? Administrative Assistant and Secretarial recruiter?

       For example:
        1. Services: generalist, serving small businesses, non-profits, and associations with services including:
            a. Traditional HR services such as policies, handbooks, orientation, compensation, recruiting, retention, etc.
            b. Non-traditional HR services such as measuring the results of the human resource services, or integrating human resource plans into the strategic process and plan
            c. Strategic Planning Services
            d. Business Advisory and Executive Coaching Services
            e. Coaching Employees toward Career Development Goals
            f. Interpersonal Skills Training
            g. Speaking Topics: Consulting, Training, Strategic Human Resources, Networking, etc.
        2. Products:
            a. Employee handbooks, employee pocket guides
            b. Compensation plans, guidelines for implementation and updating
            c. An employee selection system and customized hiring guide

d. Succession planning assessment and individualized career development plans
e. First line supervisory training, communications, listening, teambuilding, delegating, and managing from the middle of the organization.
f. Human resource function assessment, analysis of the gap between the current operations and the required or desired operations as well as priorities in making changes.

Appendix 5

Human Resources Skill Assessment

AREAS OF EXPERTISE

Skills

Indicate your level of expertise in the following skills using the rating scale below:

(3) Substantial experience or training in this area – consider it an area of expertise

(2) Some experience to this area – have working knowledge of this area

(1) Little exposure to this area – not a personal skills area

Circle Level of Expertise

1. Absenteeism control and prevention.. 3 2 1
2. Affirmative action 3 2 1
3. Assessment centers... 3 2 1
4. Attitudes and job satisfaction 3 2 1

5. Benefits administration 3 2 1
6. Benefits analysis and planning 3 2 1
7. Career development 3 2 1
8. Change management 3 2 1
9. Coaching and counseling 3 2 1
10. Collective bargaining 3 2 1
11. Communication programs 3 2 1
12. Compensation administration 3 2 1
13. Compensation analysis and planning 3 2 1
14. Compensation design 3 2 1
15. Conflict management 3 2 1
16. Culture and climate 3 2 1
17. Disabilities and Americans with Disabilities Act (ADA) compliance 3 2 1
18. Discipline and discharge 3 2 1
19. Diversity issues and training 3 2 1
20. Downsizing and layoff administration 3 2 1
21. Equal Employment Opportunity (EEO) 3 2 1
22. Employee Assistance Programs (EAP) 3 2 1
23. Employee development 3 2 1
24. Employee relations 3 2 1
25. Executive coaching 3 2 1
26. Expatriate management 3 2 1
27. Health and wellness issues at work 3 2 1
28. Ergonomics and industrial hygiene 3 2 1

29. Individual assessment 3 2 1

30. Individual coaching and feedback 3 2 1

31. Information systems 3 2 1

32. International human resources 3 2 1

33. Interviewing 3 2 1

34. Job analysis and evaluation 3 2 1

35. Job design and redesign 3 2 1

36. Leadership development 3 2 1

37. Legal issues 3 2 1

Skills

Indicate your level of expertise in the following skills using the rating scale below:

(3) Substantial experience or training in this area – consider it an area of expertise

(2) Some experience to this area – have working knowledge of this area

(1) Little exposure to this area – not a personal skills area

Circle Level of Expertise

38. Labor law 3 2 1

39. Management and executive development 3 2 1

40. Motivational systems and issues 3 2 1

41. Multi-source feedback (e.g., peers, subordinates, etc.) 3 2 1

42. Opinion surveys and morale management 3 2 1

43. Occupational Safety and Health Act (OSHA) compliance 3 2 1

44. Outplacement 3 2 1
45. Performance appraisal and management 3 2 1
46. Policy development 3 2 1
47. Process consulting and advising 3 2 1
48. Productivity improvement 3 2 1
49. Program evaluation 3 2 1
50. Project management 3 2 1
51. Quality processes and Total Quality Management (TQM) 3 2 1
52. Record keeping (personnel files) 3 2 1
53. Recruiting and job search 3 2 1
54. Reengineering business processes 3 2 1
55. Reward systems 3 2 1
56. Safety and accident prevention 3 2 1
57. Selection and staffing 3 2 1
58. Sexual harassment 3 2 1
59. Statistics and data analysis 3 2 1
60. Strategic planning and corporate strategy 3 2 1
61. Stress management 3 2 1
62. Substance abuse in the workplace 3 2 1
63. Succession planning 3 2 1
64. Survey development and research 3 2 1
65. Team building 3 2 1
66. Team design 3 2 1
67. Test administration 3 2 1
68. Test design and validation 3 2 1

69. Training and education coordination and administration 3 2 1
70. Training and education delivery 3 2 1
71. Training and education needs assessment 3 2 1
72. Training and education program design 3 2 1
73. Training and education program evaluations 3 2 1
74. Turnover control and prevention 3 2 1
75. Union avoidance 3 2 1
76. Union relations 3 2 1
77. Work and family life issues 3 2 1
78. Other: ______________________________

____

____

Skills

Indicate your level of expertise in the following skills using the rating scale below:

(3) Substantial experience or training in this area – consider it an area of expertise

(2) Some experience to this area – have working knowledge of this area

(1) Little exposure to this area – not a personal skills area

Circle Level of Expertise

1. Specialist (e.g., compensation, recruiting, etc.) 3 2 1
2. Generalist (wide range of responsibilities) 3 2 1
3. Management of specialists 3 2 1

4. Management of generalists 3 2 1
5. Management of large projects 3 2 1
6. Consulting – internal(to own organization) 3 2 1
7. Consulting – external(to other organizations) 3 2 1
8. Executive (responsible for entire HR function or large component) 3 2 1
9. Executive/administrative assistant 3 2 1
10. Other skills:____

____

Skill Preferences

Indicate the various skill domains in which you would prefer to work:

(Use numbers from skill list on pages 1, 2, and 3)

____

____

____

Appendix 6

Subcontractor Agreement

Gravett and Associates

This Agreement covers collaboration between Gravett and Associates and ____ for client ______________________________________. The lead consultant (Dr. Linda Gravett) agrees to work with you to make you as successful as possible. To ensure this, the following fully outlines our mutual expectations during our work together.

Ethics

- We value a strong ethical consideration in working with our clients and collaborators. These values and expectations are detailed below:
- As a subcontractor, you have been selected because of the level of your expertise and proven track record. This is of value to us and to our client(s). We will ensure that you receive all of the

information you need to optimize your expertise and role as subcontractor. You are responsible for communicating what you need and expect.

- You will work through the lead consultant rather than directly with the client, unless otherwise determined.
- It is expected that subcontractors will support our client-focused approach. This means that services are designed to be cost effective and value added for the client, which may not always result in using all of our services or capabilities or may at times limit billing opportunities. This also means that subcontractor work performed does not endeavor to make the client consultant dependent. Our goal is to move the client to self-sufficiency.
- Subcontractors are not permitted to solicit the client for other services the subcontractor may provide. Any additional services must be discussed and arranged through the lead consultant.
- Proposals and quotes are calculated to create the most cost-effective arrangement for both the client and lead consultant in order to achieve a value added position for both.
- Lead consultant will ensure that any pertinent information and/or feedback from the client will be communicated promptly to the subcontractor throughout the work relationship.

Confidentiality

All persons involved on this project will maintain the strictest confidentiality with regard to the client: their business strategies (marketing, management or otherwise), finances, all employment matters, personal matters, competitive information and any other proprietary information.

Intellectual Property

Any concepts developed for Gravett and Associates clients by subcontractor are the property of either the client or Gravett and Associates, whichever is agreed to during the project proposal phase of negotiations. No intellectual property shall be used by subcontractor for non-Gravett and Associates clients unless by express written mutual agreement between subcontractor and Gravett and Associates.

Payment Terms

The lead consultant agrees to pay the subcontractor monies owed within 10 (ten) working days of receipt of payment from the client. This fee is based on the attached proposal, which has been accepted by client,

____.

Signed:

______________________	___________________
Lead Consultant Gravett and Associates	Date

______________________	___________________
Subcontractor	Date

CPSIA information can be obtained at www.ICGtesting.com
Printed in the USA
LVOW010136041111

253375LV00001B/29/P